THE
TASSELS
BOOK

THE
TASSELS
BOOK

AN INSPIRATIONAL GUIDE TO TASSELS AND TASSEL-MAKING, WITH OVER 40 PRACTICAL PROJECTS

ANNA CRUTCHLEY
PHOTOGRAPHS BY TIM IMRIE

LORENZ BOOKS
LONDON • NEW YORK • SYDNEY • BATH

For Brooke and Diana Crutchley

This edition first published in 1996 by Lorenz Books

Lorenz Books is an imprint of Anness Publishing Limited
Hermes House, 88-89 Blackfriars Road, London SE1 8HA

This edition is distributed in Canada by
Raincoast Books Distribution Limited

ISBN 1 85967 222 1

Publisher: Joanna Lorenz
Senior Editor: Clare Nicholson
Photographer: Tim Imrie
Stylist: Anna Tait
Designer: Simon Balley
Illustrator: John Hutchinson
and Katie Sleight

Printed and bound in China

3 5 7 9 10 8 6 4 2

Contents

The Traditions

Tassels have a very long and illustrious history, frequently being used to indicate status and wealth as well as being a form of decoration. Throughout the centuries the furnishings of great houses have been embellished with tassels, and tassels have been, and still are, used in ceremonial costume. The Far East, India and the Arab world have all contributed to the rich variety of tassels.

Left: The variety of tassels, from simple soft tassels for cushions to tie-backs for grand interiors, is enormous.

Introduction

During the last couple of decades, those of us who are interested in textiles and interior decoration have seen how tassels and trimmings have become increasingly popular as a major feature in the design of soft furnishings and upholstery. This has occurred largely in reaction to the bare lines of the modern interiors of the 1960s and 1970s, coupled with a revival of the appreciation of good craftsmanship.

With our renewed interest in our

Right: A Balouch horse tassel which was probably worn to prevent the saddle, or carrying palette, from rubbing the horse. This meticulous piece of weaving has heavily tasselled warp ends.

national heritage, we visit stately homes to learn about the famous families who owned them, and to admire the furniture they collected, the wallpapers and curtains they commissioned, the way the four-poster beds were dressed and how tassels, braids, cords and fringes were skilfully designed and made to enhance these furnishings. We realize that we are

Left: These contemporary tassels have been made following classical designs but the modern materials and colour schemes give them a wonderfully fresh feel. (Left) A wool tassel using a curtain-pole finial as a mould. (Middle) A dip-dyed silk tassel tie-back. (Right) A cotton steeple-mould tassel tie-back.

Right: Tassels are the equivalent of jewellery for interiors. These exquisite 19th-century French tassels are absolutely crammed with detail and were probably commissioned for a palace.

looking at jewellery, but jewellery for interiors rather than dress.

Closer study of these tassels shows us that traditional skills and techniques, with a long and fascinating history, have been developed according to the fashions of time. The French word for it is passementerie – a general term covering all types of fringes, froggings and braids, for dress and interior decorations, gives the work the status it deserves.

Passementerie is a hybrid craft. It employs the talents of the cordspinner, weaver and tassel maker, each of whom works to a high level of skill and expertise. They, in turn, are answerable to the interior decorator or upholsterer who is commissioned by the owner of the house to design schemes of great taste and imagination.

What began as a simple way to finish the warp ends of woven cloth or braid, evolved over the years into status symbols for the rich and powerful, and were used extensively in both interiors and costume. Now you can make tassels too – using some of the secret techniques handed down through generations of trimmings makers!

History

The nomadic tribes of the Central and Northern Asian steppes and the Bedouin of the Arabian and Sahara deserts relied on herding animals for their livelihood. Because water and grazing were scarce the Bedouin moved their herds between oases, whilst the Asian nomads followed their sheep and goats up to the fertile, grassy steppes for the summer months. In the desert the form of transport was the camel, a useful pack animal able to exist for days without fresh water. The Asian nomads had, by 3,000 BC at least, learned to tame and harness the horses that roamed freely on the steppes. They made full use of their newly discovered speed and power to conquer neighbouring tribes.

These nomad peoples' cultures excelled in the textile arts. By necessity, they led a frugal existence, with few household and personal items to hamper their itinerant lifestyle. Those possessions, however, were beautifully and intricately made. Using the wool and hair they obtained from their herds, they developed sophisticated techniques for dyeing the fibre and for making textiles to decorate themselves, their homes and their prize animals. Their clothing was intensively embroidered and their tents were covered with handmade felt or narrow weavings. These were made on primitive "fold-up" looms which were strapped together with complex woven braids which had tasselled ends. The interior of the tent would have been carpeted with rugs and kilims, and the walls of the tent were held together with long, intricately woven, tasselled bands. Their camels and horses were hung about with embroidered braids, fringed skirts, headdresses and saddle covers, woven girths and saddlebags, and corded bridles and leads. Tassels were everywhere – punctuating these intensely colourful textiles as bindings at the end of the weaving, as finishings to beadwork, or as the full stop to a belt or camel girth.

The descendants of the Mongol and Turkic nomads moved into India in the 13th century and eventually founded the Mughal dynasty, which lasted until the 18th century. The culture of Mughal India of the 16th–18th centuries has left a vast impression on contemporary arts and

Right: A Hazara beaded tassel from Afghanistan. The beads shown here would be prized items for nomads.

crafts. In India there is a sophisticated textile tradition and elephants, horses and bulls are still ceremonially adorned with embroideries, jewellery, fringes and tassels for weddings and temple festivals.

Even today the village people of Gujerat and Rajasthan dress in costume that has changed little in style since Mughal times. Tassels called parandah are plaited into the women's long hair, and in the cities you can buy brightly coloured floss silk belts and hair ornaments with gold thread-wrapped tassels.

The Muslim descendants of the Bedouin fought the Crusaders in the cruel wars to recover the Holy Land in the 12th century. These warring excursions were also an excuse to pillage

Above: This intricately-woven bead tassel band from Afghanistan would have been used as an all-purpose strap to bind the felt covering of a nomad's tent, or to tie goods onto a donkey.

Opposite: The giving of rewards by the monarch to loyal and devoted subjects dates from the Middle Ages. This tassel forms the ties for the gown of the Royal Victorian Order, first bestowed by Queen Victoria in 1896.

Right: George III (1760-1820) wearing a fantastic tassel on his robes.

the riches of the Arab world, and it is probably in the equestrian sphere that the eastern influence was first felt. The tents erected near the battlefields were crowned with finials and flags, and hung with tassels and trimmings. The more highly decorated tents signified that they belonged to a leader of high rank.

Today, we still see tassels on the trappings of royal, military and civic regalia. Gold tassels are used on the coronation robes of British monarchs and on the mantles of the great officers of the Church and State. The Knights of the Garter, peers, judges and academic dignitaries wear intricately made tassels as part of their ceremonial dress. English university undergraduates were nicknamed "tassels" because of the black silk tassel suspended from their mortar boards.

As well as the traditional use of tassels on long braided cords for ceremonial regalia, 15th- and 16th-century portraits show how they were used on curtains, cushions and furniture. Usually made of gold thread with red or black

wool, they denote the wealth and status of the sitter, and are also a device in the artist's composition. Your eye is often drawn to the tassel, and if the artist is clever it will be at an important point in the portrait. This is what a tassel is meant to do – to draw your eye to the most important part of a scene, whether in a painting or a real interior. In the paintings of the Late Renaissance, intricate tassels

are painted with great precision, as are the satins, gauzes and velvets that cover the furniture or are draped from the doorways. Until the late 19th century, when the Impressionist painters decided that accurate representation was not the acme of a good picture, we are able to glean detailed information about the shape, size and construction of tassel design at different times in history.

The great houses of the aristocracy are now more accessible than ever, and original trimmings and tassels still exist in many of them. At Chatsworth, in Derbyshire, England, the Queen of Scots

Below: The cushions in this portrait of Empress Marie-Louise of France show the extent to which tassels were used in lavish interiors at this time.

Bedroom and Dressing Room, the Alcove Bedroom and the Wellington Bedroom are furnished with elaborate 19th-century four-poster beds and window curtaining designs that make use of contemporary hand-painted chintz drapery. The drop fringes suspended from the swags and tails at the windows match the tassel tie-backs holding the bed curtains. They are very ornate, with

different arrangements of drops, depending on whether a longer silhouette is required to accentuate the height of the tester or a shorter set of spheres at the base.

At Knole, in Kent, England, where Charles I resided before the English Civil War, the rich and elaborate four-poster beds in silk velvets and damasks mark that handsome period of design in the mid-17th century. In an inventory from Knole

Above: (Left) A 19th-century tie-back showing the armorial bearings of the City of Paris. (Right) A tassel which was designed for the bathroom of King Louis-Phillipe (1830–48) at Neuilly.

before a great sale in 1651 we learn that the value of Raphael's *Cartoons* was listed at one third of the price of a single richly embroidered green satin bed. The state bed was a phenomenon peculiar to the 17th and 18th centuries and vast amounts of money were spent building and upholstering it. These grand bedrooms epitomized the social standing and hospitality of the family, and were the venue for such events as christenings. There are many accounts of state

Above: Tassel tie-backs, mainly from the 19th century. The second from the left is an historical reproduction in green and pink silk. The second from the right is unusually decorated with fine gimp and cord lattice-work on the moulds.

bedrooms being made ready for a royal visit which – for one reason or another – never happened. It is on these state beds that the most remarkable tassels are found.

For the Victorians, who loved highly decorated and crowded interiors, tassels were *de rigueur*. Handicrafts were a particularly Victorian pursuit and there are directions for making tassels and fringing in such craft books as Thérèse de Dilmont's *Encyclopaedia of Needlework*, written as a manual for DMC which still manufactures high-quality embroidery thread today.

Of all the European countries, tassel making reached its height in France in the 17th century. The court of Louis XIV was famous for its lavish display, and the building of the Palace of Versailles provided an excuse for even greater

Below: An exquisite historical reproduction of a drop fringe, designed to be seen on swagged curtains.

extravagance. Essential furnishing accessories were tassels with shell and pear shaped moulds, and gold and silver threads mixed with crimson, yellow and brilliant blue.

The traditional companies who make tassels and trimmings in London's East End developed from the Huguenot colonization of that area in the 17th and 18th centuries. The Protestant Huguenot families fled from religious persecution in France, sailing across the English Channel in their thousands. Their skills as craftsmen, as weavers in particular, were to have a great impact on the economy and culture of Britain. Weavers settled in the Spitalfields area of East London, and were soon assimilated into British life. They wove the sumptuous figured silks that epitomize the sophisticated fashions of the 18th century. Ribbons were woven on a specially designed narrow loom, and it is these looms that are used to hand weave the braids and fringes made in trimmings workshops today.

Tassels are still made today for interior decorators by the family companies. The tassels share a common ancestry with those historically made for ceremonial dress and military regalia which, in turn, owe their origins to the decorative textile skills of the nomads of the steppes and deserts. This unbroken tradition has been obscured in recent years by the modernist style of the post-

war period. Now we are inspired again by historical interiors to give tassels the importance they deserve as the exclamation mark of contemporary interior decoration.

Above: These original and decorative tassels explore the use of paint effects on moulds. Occasionally the skirts are dip-dyed to match the moulds.

Uses of Tassels

Throughout history, tassels have been used in interior decoration to embellish window curtains and blinds, four-poster beds and upholstered furniture.

Opposite: This interior illustrates what many of us consider to be the main function of tassels; it includes curtain tie-backs, chair tassels and fringing, all of which add perfect detail to the scheme.

They have also been worn in regal, court, military, academic and clerical dress, and in legal and civic robes, to enhance the status of the wearer, and as such they play a part in our historical identity. Although cords and braids often have a practical use, at the end of the day tassels are really there to capture attention.

Right: French tassels designed c. 1810. These heavy wool tassels in beautiful shades of pink are quite complex in construction. The cord skirt is hung with squab wool tufts, and topped with a cut ruff. The moulds are carved with spirals, wound with yarn, and then a fine cord is laid in the spiral. Tiny rosettes made from uncut ruffs are positioned in the middle and hung with squab tassels. The tassels are suspended from an eight-strand cord made up of plain and double-spun strands.

Above: In recent years, the revival of interest in tassels and fringing has meant that they have been widely used as a form of embellishment in all areas of interior design. A butterfly loop is formed in the cord of these tassels, and used to give focus to a plain lampshade.

Left: Tassels are frequently used on cushions and bolsters, either with or without a matching piping cord. In the same way that you choose jewellery to enhance your clothes, tassels should also be designed to set off the soft furnishings they are seen with.

Left: Pompom and bullion tassels made out of natural cottons have been used to decorate an upholstered chair. The cord protects the seam of the upholstery and the tassels at each end are purely decorative.

Opposite: This colourful pompom blind pull was made to be seen in a window.

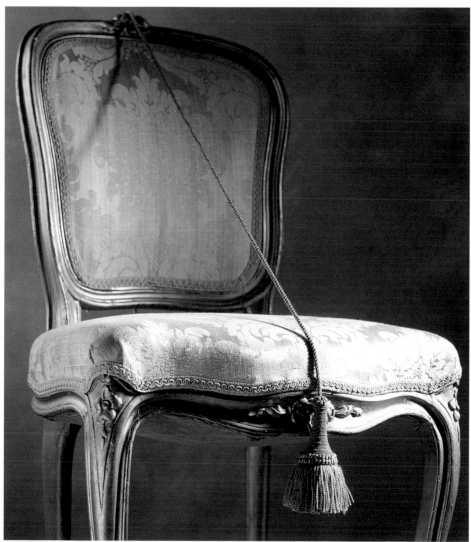

Above: Tassels are frequently used as light-pulls and bell-pulls.

Left: An elegant silk and wool tassel that was made to protect 18th-century furniture. Draped over from the back, it prevents people from sitting on the furniture.

Right: Tassels and cords are essential accessories to military musical instruments, both to strap the trumpet to the soldier, and also to denote the regiment. (Top) A silver-plated trumpet with regimental tassels and cord, 1940s. (Middle) A copy of a trumpet from 1667, made by Simon Beale. (Bottom) A silver-plated trumpet made by Henry Keat, c.1885.

Above: These tiny but intricate tassels were specially commissioned as Christmas tree decorations.

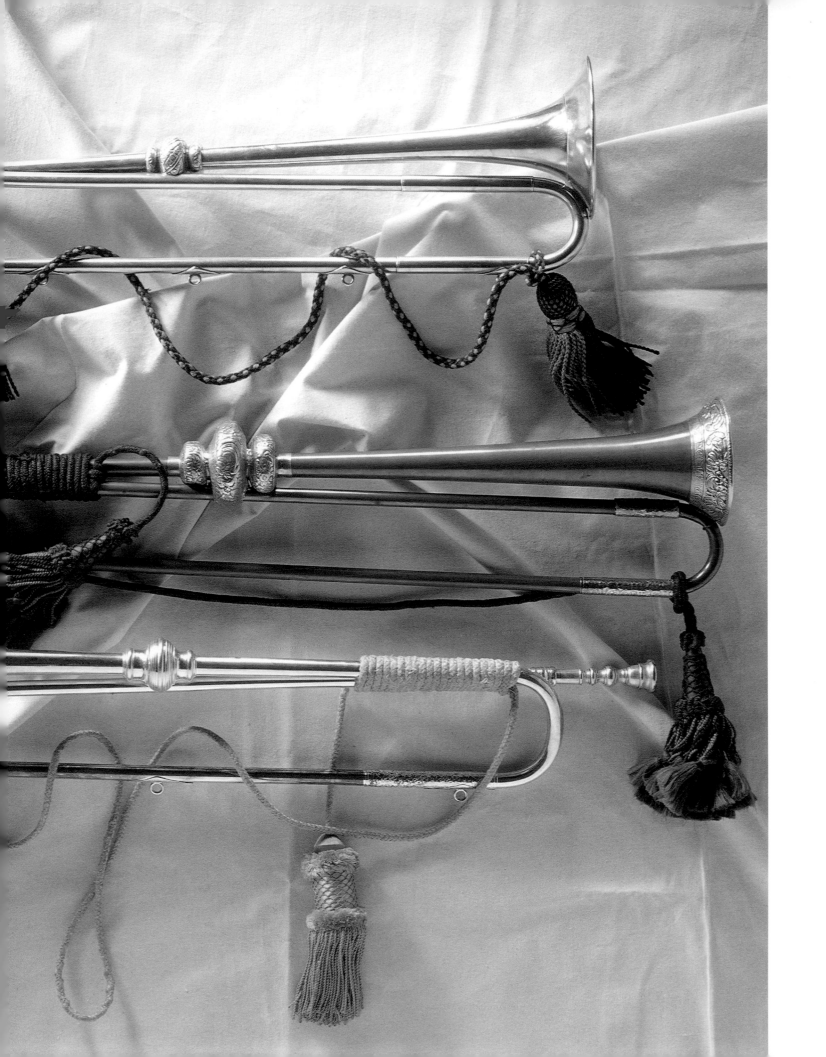

Above: Tassels are often used as fringing for furnishing fabrics, and they are also used in this way in fashion. This brightly coloured silk shawl with tasselled ends is from Turkestan.

Right: Colourful, tasselled curtain fringing and key tassels, which were designed to suit a modern interior.

Opposite: Tassels are used on all sorts of hats, such as a tam-o'-shanter, fez and mortar board. This black felt hat has a particularly spectacular long, black tassel.

Left: Tassels were first attached to fixed fans in the 17th century, but they were not added to folding fans, such as this one, until the 19th century.

Below: A 1920s yellow silk evening jacket with black velvet trim, cream embroidery and tassels, 1920s.

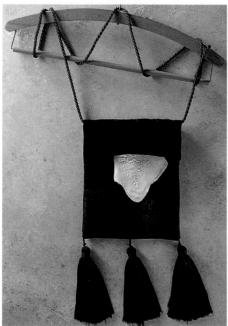

Above: Tassels give finish and weight to this silk evening bag.

The Basics

This chapter provides an introduction to the basic techniques of tassel making. The later projects refer back to these basic techniques, so as a newcomer, follow the introductory sequences on how to make a warp, spin a cord, cover a mould, and make a skirt and a ruff. You only need two specialist pieces of equipment – a warping frame and a post. Both can be replaced with home-made equivalents.

Left: Part of the joy of making tassels is that they are "over the top" forms of decoration, so do not skimp on the size of the mould or the quantity of yarn used in the skirt.

Introduction

There are three main parts to a tassel – the suspension cord, the mould and the skirt. Each of these is made as a separate entity and the whole is then put together and fastened securely. When designing tassels, it is important that the principal techniques of making each of these parts is mastered. The rest of the design process, such as which type of yarn to use, how to place the colour combinations, the shape of the tassel and its proportions is then easier to tackle. This chapter shows how to make all the basic elements of the tassels, then the following chapters show more advanced techniques and forms of decoration.

Tassels are normally used to embellish furnishings and fabrics in specifically designed interiors. Their colours are chosen to enhance the fabrics on which they will be seen and their style to suit the period of the room or its furniture. It is worth taking time to colour-match a fabric and then to plan where those colours should be placed on the tassel, and in what proportions. If a curtain fabric is mainly crimson with a bit of grey, a tassel tie-back made mainly of grey with a little crimson will stand out well. Sometimes, when the yarn shades available do not match the fabric exactly, you have to decide which way to go with your choice – lighter or darker, more towards blue or orange, and so on. You can mix more than one shade of crimson

or grey to achieve the overall colour, and this will give depth to the tassel colouring. In general, it is best to go for a richer and slightly brighter effect when matching up to a fabric, so that the tassel will stand out from its background. The range of textures and colours of yarns on the market today is extensive. It is always useful to have a range of spools of yarn in front of you so that you can wind them round your fingers to test whether colour combinations work well together.

Above: Rich in colour and texture, these simple chenille tassels have been added to cushion corners.

Opposite: Glittery, fun tassels made from metallic and slinky synthetic threads or from pleated paper can be used to jazz up gift wrappings.

Equipment and Materials

Described here are the equipment and materials that you require to make the tassels in this book. Very little special equipment is required but you will need to obtain the threads and yarns from specialist suppliers. These are listed in the back of the book.

EQUIPMENT

Warping frames and posts are available from specialist suppliers, but it would be quite easy to get a carpenter to make these. They need to be strong and sturdy and the pegs must fit firmly into the holes. If further equipment is needed for a particular project then it is listed on that page.

Warping frame A warp is a group of threads of even length and tension, used to make the suspension cord, the skirt and for covering the mould of a tassel. The length of warps needed for each part of the tassel will vary, for example, a cord might need a warp of 1m (39in) while a skirt might need a warp of between 5 and 15m (5½ and 16½yd). To prepare the warps, a frame is used to calculate the length accurately, and to lay the threads together in order. The warping frame is generally

made of wood with pegs at intervals up both sides. The threads are then wound over the pegs. The warping frame in this book will go up to 11m (12yd). The alternative to a frame is either a long garden, or corridor. You will need to hook the yarns around two immobile objects, such as the post of a washing line. The spools can be threaded onto a knitting needle, and carried up and down between the posts.

Warping post A warping post is made of two pieces of dowelling approximately 23cm (9in) apart attached to a wooden base. The warping post is clamped tightly to a sturdy table in front of you while you are working. It is an essential tassel-making tool which is used as a levering post when binding cords and tassel moulds very tightly, and is also used to store warps when covering the tassel mould. It is easy to make, but must be very strong as

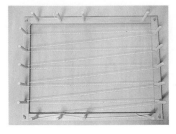

Above: A warping frame

you need to pull hard on it when working.

Hand drill A hand drill with a cuphook attached firmly in the chuck is an essential tool for making cords. A cuphook can be bought from any hardware store. When making cords, hook one end of the warp over the warping post and the other over the cuphook. The drill is used to spin the warp ready to make a cord.

Cordless electric drill An electric drill with a cuphook is used for the same purpose as a hand drill, and is particularly useful if you are spinning up very long warps. It should have a reverse action.

Cabler This is a specialist tool for spinning cords, and it

twists up to four strands at the same time, so it is particularly good for three- and four-strand cords.

Scissors Scissors must be sharp. A small pair with a good point and a large, fine-bladed pair are essential.

Wire snips These are needed to cut the wire which is used

KEY

❶ Warping frame

❷ Single warping post

❸ Double warping post

❹ Hand drill

❺ Cordless electric drill, with cuphook in the chuck

❻ Cabler

❼ Small sharp scissors

❽ Large scissors

❾ Wire snips

❿ Round-nosed pliers

⓫ Skirt boards

⓬ G-clamp

⓭ Comb

⓮ Tape measure

⓯ Mattress needle and a selection of knitting needles

for the skirts, ruffs and cords.

Round-nosed pliers Pliers are useful for twisting up the skirt wires tightly.

Skirt boards Tassel skirts are made on boards. These come in a wide range of sizes. Shop-sold boards are made out of wood but you can also make your own out of cardboard.

G-clamp A g-clamp is needed to secure the warping post firmly to your work surface.

Comb This is used to tidy up the tassel skirt.

Tape measure You will need a tape measure to calculate the lengths of the warps you are working with.

Needles A selection of long needles, including tapestry needles with blunt ends, is used to cover tassel moulds.

Knitting needles These are useful for separating the warps when you are making three- and four-strand cords, and also for making ruffs.

Kettle When your tassel is complete it is a good idea to hold it over a steaming kettle to fluff up the yarns. Be careful not to scald yourself.

MATERIALS

When making tassels the variety of threads for you to choose from is enormous. There are cottons, wools, silks and synthetic fibres.

The materials listed for each project give the specific make and colour of the threads. When starting it is advisable to use the specified materials and choose the projects which do not use expensive threads such as silk. Before you start working with the threads, make your warp (see Basic Techniques). The warps are then transferred to a spool ready for use.

The yarns used throughout the book have a count number. This number indicates the thickness of the yarn, and its length per kilogram or pound. The function of the count system is firstly so that the spinner can ensure a specific quality of yarn, and secondly so that the user can calculate the quantity needed for a project. Count systems vary according to the type of fibre used and where the fibre was spun, so a Swedish linen count will be

different from a British wool count. Along with the count of the yarns, we have given the size of the package available from the supplier and the approximate length of thread this will give you. The instructions given in each project relate to the specific counts in the materials list. With a little experience you will be able to substitute yarns of a different count, adding or subtracting quantities as appropriate.

KEY

1. Madeira Tanne cotton 30
2. Madeira Sticku rayon 30
3. Madeira metallic thread
4. Appleton's crewel wool
5. Bocken's and Borg's 16/1's and 16/2's linens
6. Texere 2/27's silk
7. Gimp or bourdon cord
8. Fine jute yarn
9. Strong polyester thread
10. Moulds
11. Beads
12. Galvanized wire, 1mm (0.039in)
13. Strong-impact adhesive

Madeira Tanne cotton 30
This cotton yarn is used throughout the book. It is a fine, mercerized thread, just slightly thicker than normal sewing cotton. It comes in a wide range of colours, so it is easy to match up to fabrics in the home. It is sold in 25g (1oz) spools of about 625m (650yd) per spool.

Madeira polyester and rayon threads These are man-made fibres that come in similar counts to Tanne 30. These threads are quite inter-changeable. They are sold in 25g (1oz) spools of about 625m (684yd) per spool.

Madeira metallics This synthetic metallic thread is sold in most good haberdashery stores. It comes in 50g (2oz) spools with about 625m (684yd) per spool.

Appleton's crewel wool This fine plied wool is commonly used for needlepoint tapestry and crewel embroidery. It comes in a fantastic range of about 500 shades, and looks particularly good when matching up to a wool fabric. Haberdashery and embroidery shops stock a wide selection of shades, and will be able to order the larger 25g (1oz) hanks.

William Hall's 1200/2's rayon This rayon thread is a slightly thicker yarn than the Madeira threads. It is normally used for weaving and knitting, but hangs well and is ideal for tassels. It is available in large spools of 500g (1lb 2oz) and there are 5500m per 500g (6000yd per 1lb 2oz).

Bocken's and Borg's 16/2's linens Swedish linen is the best quality and the smoothest linen thread. It has a wonderful natural look but it is also has a rather sophisticated feel. Linen thread hangs very well so is ideal for tassels with longer cut skirts. The Swedish linens come in 125g (4oz) and 250g (10oz) cops or cones, and there is approximately 2300m per 500g (2500yd per lb 2oz). These are available from weaving suppliers.

Texere SS30 2/27's silk The weaving silk used here is probably twice as thick as a sewing cotton. This silk comes in 250g or 500g (10oz or 20oz) cops or cones, and there is approximately 420m per 25g (460yd per oz). It is normally available from weaving suppliers.

Gimp Gimp comprises a core yarn that is wound on the outside with a good quality yarn. This is a rayon gimp, available from specialist embroidery suppliers.

Fine jute yarn This is good for making rustic-looking tassels. Another alternative is thin garden twine.

Strong polyester thread This strong, almost unbreakable thread is used for binding and tying throughout the book. Nylon button or top-stitching thread is good too. These are available from all good haberdashery shops.

Tassel moulds Moulds form the central core of tassels, and it is at this point that the cord and the skirt are attached. Because the craft is fairly new moulds can be difficult to get hold of. The ones used in the projects are available by mail order from the author (see list of suppliers). Alternatively, templates have been given at the back of the book. Any good woodturner should be able to turn them for you and they can be made out of any type of wood. The templates show the moulds at the size they should be used for the projects. You can make them larger or smaller but this will affect the amount of yarn required. Resin moulds on the market are not as good because they are very lightweight.

Beads Available from specialist bead shops and haberdashery stores, beads are used for decoration and they can also be covered with yarn. If they are going to be covered, look for beads that have a large central hole.

Galvanized wire You will need wire of about a 1mm (0.039in) thickness to attach heavy cords to tassel moulds. You will also need thinner florist's wire which is about 0.37mm (0.014in) for making skirts and ruffs.

Glue Use a very strong glue to roll the tassel moulds and then a lighter clear glue for minor adhesions. Also have some masking tape to secure the ends of warps if you are making a multi-strand cord.

The Parts of the Tassel

1

Tassels normally comprise three parts – the cord, the mould and the skirt – and there is a variety of techniques for embellishing each part. However intricate the design of the tassel, in the end there must be balance in both the colour and the decoration. The proportions of a tassel mirror those of the human figure, the skirt (or legs) being normally a quarter to one-third again the length of the mould (or torso).

1 THE CORD

The function of the cord is to suspend the tassel. It is attached to the tassel by being threaded or wired through the mould. Although here we are looking at the cord first, it may in fact be designed last in order to balance the detailing on the rest of the tassel. A cord normally comprises two, three or four strands of yarn.

2 THE MOULD

For most of the tassels in this book you will be using a mould. The mould is usually a turned wood shape with a central hole. It is either rolled with a fine cord, or gimp, covered with yarn or painted. Traditional detailing includes striping (where fine Z and S cords are placed vertically on the mould) netting (where a find cord net is applied) and snailing (where cords are crossed around the mould in an intricate trellised pattern). The skirt is attached to the "waist" of the mould.

3 THE SKIRT

The skirt is the fringing that hangs down from the mould. There are two basic types of skirt: a cut skirt which is made of loose yarn that has been cut and trimmed, and a bullion skirt which is made of a highly spun warp, or gimp, that twists back on itself as the skirt is made to give a folded loop. Careful placing of colour, in tiers or in panels, helps to balance the skirt. Skirts can be decorated with overbullions – thicker looped cords that are spaced around the skirt, and sometimes have tufts at the bottom. They can also be trellised, hung with jasmins (cascades of drooping four-leaf gimp flowers), drops of covered beads or pompoms, or tufted to give the tassel a bulkier look.

4 THE RUFF

This is a decorative device to cover up the joins where different parts of the tassel meet, such as the cord and the mould, and the mould and the skirt.

Basic Techniques

The basic techniques show in detail the process of making a tassel. To understand how to make a tassel, work through each of the sections before going on to any of the projects which are more elaborate. When working through the projects in the later chapters you will need to refer back to the basic techniques.

WARPS

Fundamental to the construction of tassels is the technique of preparing lengths of groups of threads. These threads are called a warp – a warp is a length of multiple threads all of the same length and tension. Each warp consists of several threads and each thread is referred to as an "end", for example, a warp of 20 ends has 20 threads. For each tassel you need several warps of different lengths, and these lengths are given in the instructions at the start of each project. The weavers and tassel makers in trimmings workshops both make warps, for weaving braids and fringes as well as for covering moulds and making tassel skirts. The warping frame shown here is ideal for home use.

If you are working through one of the projects in the book follow the specifications for the length of warp you need. If you are practising for the basic techniques, make a warp of 20 ends of 5m (5½yd). In the illustrations you will see that the 5m (5½yd) warp reaches half way up the 11m (12yd) warping frame.

Making a warp

1 Take thick string in a contrasting colour to your warp and tie an overhand knot to make a loop. As a guide, mark the string every metre or yard with a pen.

2 Slide the knot over one of the corner pegs, then wind as much of the string onto the frame as you need for your warp.

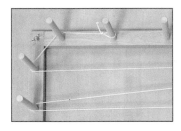

3 Zigzag from one side of the frame to the other. Tie a second knot in the end of the string and loop it over the last peg.

4 Take your warp threads and follow the path made by the string around the warping board.

5 At the end, turn and trace the same path back.

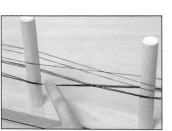

6 Make a cross at the end, to help with counting the threads. Count the number of threads at the cross.

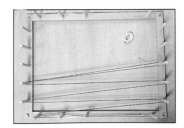

7 Finish off by tying a knot. Wind the warp off the frame into a ball or onto a bobbin.

CORDSPINNING

Cordspinning forms the basis of tassel making. The cordspinner's skill can produce anything from fine net twines 1mm (0.039in) thick to chunky barrier ropes of 5cm (2in) diameter. At its most basic, a cord is made of two groups of threads twisted individually in the same direction, and then twisted together in the opposite direction. Tassels are usually made of two, three or four strands, but within this there are many variations.

Simple cords are easy to spin, using little more equipment than a cuphook in the chuck of a good hand drill. One step up on this is a cordless electric drill with a reverse action. The cordspinner shown on page 35 was made especially by an engineer and has four hooks that spin simultaneously. For good results, make sure that your strands are exactly the same length, and that you twist up each strand the same amount to form an even cord. With a hand drill, count the number of times you turn the handle. With a cordless electric drill, place a marker on an adjoining table and spin up to the same point for each strand.

Before you start work, wind some strong (ie almost unbreakable) polyester thread in a figure-of-eight about a dozen times around a warping post. This thread is used constantly during tassel making for binding and tying. It is good to use a contrasting colour to the tassel yarns.

Two-strand cord

MATERIALS

■ For the two-strand cord you will need two warps of 20 ends x 1.1m (42in); for the three-strand cord you will need three warps of 20 ends x 1.1m (42in); for the four-strand cord you will need four warps of 20 ends x 1.1m (42in).

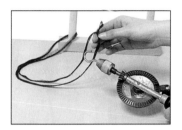

1 Place the first warp on the warping post. Place the other end over the end of the cuphook on the hand drill.

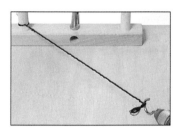

2 Twist the warp up tightly, counting the number of times you turn the handle of the drill.

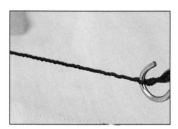

3 To get a nice, tightly spun cord you need to twist it up until it looks wriggly, and just about to kink.

4 Tape the twisted warp to the table, leaving the loop free at the end. Twist up the second warp in the same direction, the same number of turns on the handle.

5 With both strands back on the cuphook, twist them together in the opposite direction.

6 The cord should be firmly twisted. Knot both ends and allow any overtwist to fall out by suspending the cord.

Three-strand cord

For three- and four-strand cords you need to have a friend working with you, particularly for longer cords. You will need assistance to hold the knitting needles in place, so that the cord spins up in the correct colour order.

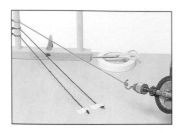

1 Twist up each of the three strands separately.

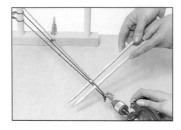

2 Ask a friend to hold the knitting needles as shown.

3 Slip the knitting needles up the strands as the cord is plied.

4 Knot the ends of the cord when the spinning is completed.

Four-strand cord, using a cabler

1 For the four-strand cord, slip the stopper into the head of the cabler.

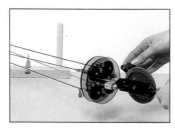

2 Twist up each of the four strands.

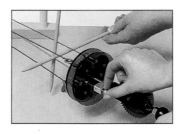

3 Ask a friend to insert the knitting needles in a cross. Release the stopper.

4 Turn the handle in the same direction, slipping the needles in front of the twist as you spin.

5 The needles ensure the correct colour order as the cord is spun.

6 Bind the ends with strong polyester thread to prevent the cord unravelling.

THE MOULD

There are two basic methods of treating the tassel mould. The first is covering, in which a group of yarns is looped vertically onto the mould and laced by a strong thread on the inside. The second is rolling, in which a cord or gimp is wound and glued round the mould, from top to bottom. Use a strong-impact adhesive, which does not dry too quickly. If the mould has straight sides and only a small amount of shaping it is normally covered, whereas a more rounded, convex or concave shape is rolled.

Covering a mould

During the covering process you must maintain the tension on the polyester thread. Place your second or middle finger on the thread while you loop the yarn over the warp and back through the hole. When you are turning the mould, keep the thread taut.

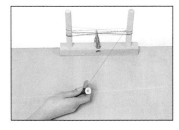

1 Wind strong polyester thread in a figure-of-eight round the warping post.

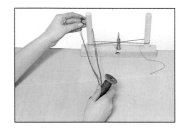

2 Make a warp of 1.1m (42in) and hook the end over the post. Take 25cm (10in) of the warp, untwist it and flick the strands.

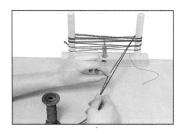

3 Wind the warp in a figure-of-eight round the post. Repeat every 25cm (10in) until all of the warp is on the warping post.

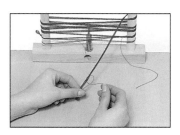

4 Cut about 60cm (24in) of polyester thread and tie a half-hitch knot around the warp (see page 44).

5 Tie a second half-hitch knot to secure it.

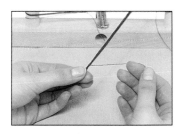

6 Tighten the knot and snip off the ends.

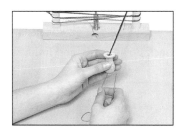

7 Thread the other end of the polyester thread through a tapestry needle that is longer than your tassel mould. Pass the needle up the mould from bottom to top.

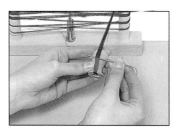

8 Turn the mould so that it lies with the warp on top. Use the needle to spread out the warp.

Continued overleaf

BINDING

Binding the mould after the skirt has been attached has three functions. It hides the top of the skirt, finishes off the shape of the tassel and provides a base for the ruff. You can use thread straight from the spool, or you can spin up a fine cord.

1 Wind the thread round the mould and skirt, filling in the smallest part of the waist. Turn the mould as you go to ensure a flat, even wrapping.

2 Stitch in the thread with a sewing needle.

3 Snip off the ends of the thread.

MAKING A RUFF

Wherever the different parts of a tassel meet – between the cord and mould, and the mould and skirt – there are often wires, bindings and yarn ends which need to be covered. A ruff conceals these loose ends and also accentuates the shape of the tassel. Ruffs are tricky to make and it takes a little time to get used to making one tightly.

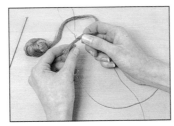

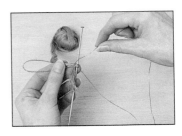

1 Cut a 1.1m (42in) length of 0.37mm (0.014in) wire, fold it in half and make a loop in the folded end.

2 Insert the warp between the two halves of wire and fasten in place by wrapping the wire around once.

3 Place the wire over a knitting needle, with one wire in front and one behind. Twist the warp away.

4 Bring the back wire round to the front.

5 Swap it with the front wire, which then wraps tightly round the back.

6 Pull the wires tightly as you continue to make the ruff in this way.

FITTING AND ATTACHING A RUFF

You may need to bind the tassel waist a little to give a nice, flat belt for the ruff to sit on.

1 Pull the ruff to tighten the wires.

2 With the wires pointing down, place the ruff at the top of the tassel waist.

3 Wrap the ruff carefully round the tassel mould to check it will go exactly twice or three times round. It is better to make it longer than your estimate, as it is easier to undo rather than add more.

4 Take the wires round to the other side of the tassel, and twist them tightly. Tweak the ruff round so that it looks like concentric circles and not a spiral.

ATTACHING THE CORD

1 Make the cord into a loop and tie an overhand knot at the end. Snip off the ends.

2 Using a long sewing needle and strong polyester thread, tie round the cord. Pass the needle through the mould, pulling the cord behind the thread.

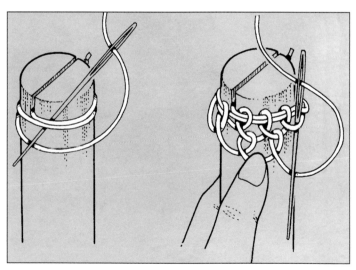

TIDYING THE SKIRT

1 Cut through the loops with a pair of sharp scissors. Comb the skirt, then trim it carefully.

2 Hang the tassel. Comb it again and even out the level of the skirt.

Above: Detached buttonhole stitch is the stitch used for making a net to cover the mould in three of the projects: the linen blind pull, the tartan drawstring bag and the tassel with cut ruff.

Cords

The cords used in tassel making may not be the focal point in the design but they are fundamental to the whole process of planning a tassel. As well as being used to suspend the tassel, they also serve as detailings on the mould, as bindings and for tufted skirts. The possible variations in the design of cords are enormous. Once you have mastered the basic technique, cordspinning can become an absorbing interest in its own right.

Left: A selection of fine cords made on the ropewalk by spinning coloured yarn over a core of cheaper cotton.

Introduction

In this chapter we start at the beginning, spinning up the cords and simple twines that will give the most basic tassel a crisp and professional finish. At the end of the chapter are projects that explore more complex cordspinning processes such as plain and double-spun suspension cords, and S and Z striping.

The principles of cordspinning begin with understanding about the direction of the twist in a cord and determining how to spin the separate strands in order to achieve that twist. Basically, a cord can be spun clockwise or anti-clockwise. If you look at a cord that has been spun clockwise, the direction of the twist is described as S, and an anti-clockwise spin as Z (see diagrams shown below).

Further to this, it follows that if you are making a two-strand cord, and you start by spinning up each strand in the S direction, you will then have to ply them together in the opposite direction – which will be Z – to achieve a stable structure. The reverse also works – spin up your two strands Z to begin with, and then ply them S. S and Z spun cords can be used together in the same tassel to achieve a chevron effect, such as in the vertical stripings in the African Pod tassel on page 66.

In trimmings workshops, cords are spun in long, narrow rooms. The wall or floor is usually marked out in metres or yards, so that the spinner can measure out the strands and spin them in the correct ratios needed for plying up into cords of a required length. With your own spinning, it is important to be methodical and precise to achieve the best results.

S twist   Z twist

Right: These thick covered cords would either be used as barrier ropes or as tie-backs on heavy curtains. (Front) Pairs of strands of threads have been cabled and then four cables spun together, creating a double-spun cord. (Back) A white and red strand have been cabled and then spun together with two red strands to create a double-spun and plain cord.

Above: Tassels have always played a part in ecclesiastical dress, and this tassel was probably used as part of a vestment tie. The moulds are covered in silver leaf and all the fine yarns used for the netting over the mould, the skirt and the cord are silk threads wrapped in silver. The cord comprises a core of yarn over which the silver thread is interlaced in a diagonal criss-cross.

Above: These elegant tassel tie-backs incorporate many parts prepared by a cordspinner. The tassels on the left comprise a mould rolled with gimp and striped with cords, and on the right the moulds have been snailed with flat, covered vellums. The tassels have looped yarn skirts from which tufts are suspended. Both tie-backs have a knotted embrace made of a four-strand cord.

Right: This wool tassel uses cordspinning processes throughout, and the richness of the colour is brought out by using two very close shades of dark pink. The steeple mould is rolled with gimps in both pinks, and the skirt is made of cabled (ie double-spun) bullion.

Soft Tassel

This is the basic soft tassel, made without a tassel mould – you have probably made this kind of tassel before. Soft tassels come in many different sizes and weights of yarn; here we have a key tassel in cotton yarn, in a striking colour combination of lime green and black. The basic cordspinning includes making a suspension cord and a fine, crisp twine for binding the tassel. Both should be spun tightly for the smartest effect. Soft tassels are very easy to produce and a key tassel like this would be a perfect present. Try using different colours with black for a set of co-ordinated tassels.

Suspension cord: make a two-strand cord using two warps of 20 ends x 60cm (24in) in green. Spin them up to make a cord about 50cm (20in) long. Knot the ends together.

Binding: make a two-strand cord using two warps of 4 ends x 2m (2¼yd) in green. Spin them up to make a fine twine about 1.3m (1½yd) long.

Tassel: clamp the warping post to the table, in front of you, and wind both yarns together round it 600 times for the thickness required for the tassel. You will probably lose count, so have a length of yarn or string ready to tie round the yarn after every 20 loops. You will then only need to count back to the last tie marker if you lose your place.

1 Place the warp on top of a length of polyester thread. Then put the cord on top of the warp so that the knot is just 1cm (½in) left of centre.

2 Tie the polyester thread tightly, pulling the skirt up to wrap evenly round the suspension cord.

3 Cut through the looped ends of the skirt. Turn the skirt over.

4 Carefully comb the skirt into place. Make a loop with the fine twine.

5 Working from top to bottom, wrap the twine tightly round the skirt. Pass the end through the loop.

6 Pull the twine up into the binding. Snip the ends off close, to make them invisible.

7 Make a loop in one strand of the suspension cord.

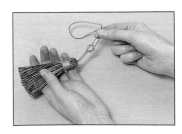

8 Pass the cord through the loop and tighten up.

Butterfly Tuft

MATERIALS

- 25g (1oz) of fine slub silk yarn

- 1 spool of Bocken's 16/1's blue linen 134 and unbleached linen

- Clear glue

- Standard equipment

*T*his simple design is called a tuft. It is made in fine linen and slub silk yarns, the linen giving it the body it needs for its size. You can also make little tufts to stud cushions or headboards, using any of the cotton yarns in this book. It is fun matching up yarn shades to a furnishing fabric and co-ordinating the tufts to give your home that extra bit of personal attention. Bind the middle of the tuft tightly, so that the yarns do not come loose.

Suspension cord: make a two-strand cord using one warp of 21 ends x 1m (39in) from a mixture of the fine slub silk, blue linen and unbleached linen. Knot the ends together.

1 Take all the yarns together and wind them round an 8.5cm (3½in) skirt board. Be careful to wind the yarns neatly, at the same angle. Wind them round the board 100 times.

2 Knot the ends of the yarns together, in the middle of the board. Slip the yarns carefully off the board.

3 Working quickly, bind the middle of the tuft tightly.

4 Loop the suspension cord round the tuft and join the ends with a small dab of glue. Open out the tuft.

Left: Pompoms are another easy tassel to make. This cotton pompom tassel has been used to embellish a washbag.

Squab Tassels

*T*his beautiful Kashmiri crewel-embroidered cushion needed a cord and tassels to finish it off. Two different cords have been used: a four-strand cord for the piping and two-strand cords for suspending the tassels. The wool stitching on the cushion has been matched with crewel embroidery wools to give a very subtle effect. Your cushion may be a different shape to this one but the quantities given should be plenty. Wool is best for these interestingly shaped squab tassels as it puffs up nicely. Wind the hanks of wool into balls before you start. See page 148 for instructions on how to attach the cords to the cushion.

MATERIALS

- 2 x 25g (1oz) hanks of Appleton's crewel embroidery wools, in each of the following colours: dark flame red 209, dull mauve 931, honeysuckle yellow 693, mid-blue 153, peacock blue 643 and terracotta 123

- Strong polyester thread

- Standard equipment

Piping: make a four-strand cord using two warps of 30 ends x 3m (3¼yd) in each strand. Strand A is colours 209 and 931 mixed, strand B is 693, strand C is 153 and 643 mixed, and strand D is 123. Ask a friend to run two knitting needles up the strands in a cross just in front of the ply, so that the colour sequence does not slip.

Suspension cord: make three two-strand cords using warps of 8 ends x 3.5m (3¾yd). Cord A is 209 and 931 mixed, cord B is 693 and cord C is 153 and 643 mixed. Make four loops from each cord.

Tassels: make a warp of 250 ends x 70cm (28in) for each set of four tassels, using the same colour combinations as for the cords.

1 Take one of the tassel warps and place a cord loop over it, 2cm (¾in) from the end. Bind with strong thread.

2 Bind the warp again with polyester thread 4cm (1½in) farther up.

3 Turn the warp over, spread it equally round the cord, and bind with strong thread.

4 Cut across the wool warp. Try to keep the cut as straight as possible.

5 Make a broader binding, using wool in a contrasting colour.

6 Pull up the cord loop, which will squash the tassel to make the squab shape.

7 Tie a knot in the loop. Make three more tassels from this warp. Repeat for the other warps.

8 Thread the tassels onto the cushion cord. Stitch three tassels, one of each colour, on each corner.

Green Jute Tassels

*T*assels to hang in your garden! They look wonderful in a small patio crammed with terracotta flowerpots. Use them to hold your runnerbean poles together in a wigwam, or sling them over verandah railings. The garden twine has been treated to delay rotting, but these tassels will fade very gracefully. You can dip the moulds in wood preserver to start with for added protection. The quantities given are for making one tassel. If you wish to make a pair, simply double the materials.

MATERIALS

- 6 rolls of green jute twine, available at garden centres

- 0.37mm (0.014in) galvanized wire

- Mould, see page 153

- Reusable adhesive

- Strong-impact adhesive

- Strong polyester thread

- Standard equipment

Suspension cord: make a three-strand cord using three warps of 6 ends x 1m (39in) in jute. Bind the ends.

Mould: take two lengths of twine 6m (6½yd) long. S spin then Z ply the strands.

Twist each length in the same direction as the original twine (probably S), and ply Z.

Skirt: make a warp of 4 ends x 15m (16½yd), using a 20cm (7¾in) skirt board. This should make 35 tags.

1 To roll the mould, place a knitting needle inside it and secure with a little reusable adhesive. Roll the mould, stopping at the neck. Do not cut the remainder of the twine off yet.

2 Wrap the skirt round the mould. Glue the top of the skirt liberally. Take the rest of the twine left after rolling the mould, and continue to roll over the skirt to form a binding.

3 Stitch in the end of the twine. Cut and trim the skirt. Take the suspension cord through the mould and knot the ends to secure.

Left: These pretty tassels are also made of jute, using the same method as the Soft Tassel on page 52.

Jute Tassel

*J*ute is a very forgiving fibre to use for tassels – it always looks crisp and is easy to manipulate. The natural texture sets off many modern furnishing fabrics and looks right in simple interiors. This tassel has the distinctive feature of a three-strand cord which is formed into a clover leaf. The pompom is great fun to make. Jute works well cut and steamed for pompoms, or for the cut ruffs later in this book. The twines look best tightly twisted, but do not overtwist or the jute may kink or even snap – experiment with a short length first.

MATERIALS

- 50g (2oz) of fine jute yarn
- 0.37mm (0.014in) galvanized wire
- Mould, see page 154
- Strong-impact adhesive
- Reusable adhesive
- Strong polyester thread
- Hammer
- Standard equipment

Suspension cord: make a three-strand cord using three warps each of 6 ends x 1m (39in). Spin the jute in the same direction as it was spun originally to stop it disintegrating. Jute is usually Z spun, so spin S and then ply Z. Bind the ends quickly.

Mould: make a two-strand cord using two warps of 2 ends x 2.5m (2¾yd). S spin each strand, then Z ply together. Bind each end quickly, before the cord unravels.

Skirt: make a warp of 6 ends x 9.6m (10½yd), using a 9.5cm (3¾in) board. Make 48 tags.

1 Glue the mould liberally and roll with the fine cord. Use a knitting needle, secured with a little reusable adhesive, to rotate the mould.

2 Take the skirt and wind it around the mould. Then bind tightly round the skirt waist, as shown. It should go round exactly twice.

3 Knot the ends of the suspension cord to make a loop. Using a sewing needle and polyester thread, take the cord through the tassel.

4 Shape the suspension cord into the first loop of the clover leaf.

5 Make the second and third loops of the clover leaf, then bind the three loops tightly with polyester thread.

6 To make the pompom, wrap jute yarn round your fingers 50 times. Slip the yarn off your fingers and bind the centre with polyester thread.

7 Cut the loops of the pompom, open it up and hammer it. Steam the pompom over a boiling kettle to fluff it up.

8 Trim the pompom, then steam it again and stitch to the clover leaf.

Linen Blind-pull

Throw out those old plastic toggles on nylon cords and replace them with these handsome linen blind-pulls instead. They look good hanging in your window from outside as well as inside, and they make a satisfying "thud thud" when they knock against the windowpane, instead of that irritating rattle. This design would also make an excellent light-pull.

The tassel has a three-strand cabled cord for strength and a netted top. The whole tassel needs to be very firm, with tight bindings, as it will have to take a lot of wear and tear. Linen yarn has a nice, heavy feel which is very suitable for this project.

MATERIALS

- 1 spool of Bocken's 16/1's linen, red 766

- Strand of wool

- Strong polyester thread

- 1.5cm (⅝in) diameter wooden dowel and hacksaw

- Standard equipment

Suspension cord: make a three-strand cord using three warps, each 10 ends x 1.5m (1¾yd). S twist the first warp, then loop it round the post, attach it to the drill and Z ply. Repeat for the next two warps. Twist up each strand, continuing the Z twist.

Ply all three strands together S, using a knitting needle to control the sequence.

Net: make a two-strand cord using two warps of 2 ends x 2.25m (2½yd). Spin up S and ply Z. Twist up both warps exactly the same number of times.

1 To make the skirt, wind the yarn round a warping post 600 times. To help with the counting, tie a strand of wool every 50 warps or so.

2 Cut the warp, place it on the table, and tie the suspension cord about 1cm (½in) below the centre. Fold the warp over evenly and bind with polyester thread.

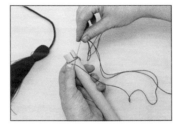

3 Make a cut in the top of the wooden dowel to create a slit. For the net, wind the twine twice round the dowel. Start stitching using detached buttonhole stitch (see page 47).

4 Make ten stitches round and space them out evenly before starting the second row. Position the last stitch quite near the end and use the same size stitch when you start the second row.

5 After eight rows, slip your needle into each loop to finish off. This last row forms a drawstring.

6 Slip the net off the dowel and onto the tassel. Pull the top end of the twine to tighten the net.

7 Stitch the twine into the tassel head and cut.

8 Pull the bottom end of the twine, wrap it twice round the tassel and stitch in.

Chunky Cord Tassel

*T*his is an inventive and wonderfully crazy tassel. The cords are manipulated in an original way, first spiralled round a wadding tube and then unravelled to form the skirt. To begin with, the whole thing appears to be upside down until you turn the cords over the wadding. The chainette ribbon is a dip-dyed, hollow tube, which is stuffed and then ruched to give an extraordinary texture. Bullion fringing found on a local market stall was stitched between the cords to add weight and decoration to the tassel head.

MATERIALS

■ 125g (4½oz) of Bocken's 16/2's linen, in three colours: red 478, gold 101 and lime 906

■ 1 cone of Texere dip-dyed chainette ribbon

■ 2m (2¼yd) of chunky knitting wool

■ 23cm x 12cm (9in x 4¾in), x 3cm (1¼in) of thick wadding

■ Strong polyester thread

■ 1m (39in) of gold bullion fringing

■ Standard equipment

Suspension cord: make a three-strand cord using three warps of 30 ends x 1.7m (2yd) in each of the linen colours: red, gold and lime. Twist them up into a three-strand cord.

Tassel cords: make a two-strand cord using one warp of 40 ends x 2m (2¼yd) in each colour. Spin up one warp, take it off the post, and pass it round the post and onto the drill. Spin up in the opposite direction. The cord should be about 90cm (35in). Bind the ends and trim to three equal lengths. Repeat for the two other colours.

1 Cut 6 x 4m (4¼yd) lengths of ribbon. Thread the chunky wool through the ribbon, gathering it up as you go to give 22cm (8¾in) of ruched cord.

2 Position the tassel cords round the suspension cord, then bind on the red, gold, and lime cords in sequence. Attach two strands of the ruched cord between the red and gold cords.

3 Take the piece of wadding and wrap it around the tassel cords. Stitch in place.

4 Bring the cords over the wadding and round the tassel as shown, and stitch down. Spiral the ruched cords as you position them.

5 Stitch the bullion fringing between the red and lime cords. Bind all the cords at the bottom of the tassel head.

6 Stitch the cords together. Unravel the skirt, then steam and comb to straighten.

African Pod

*S*ome of the best tassels are really just shapes, wound with twines and hung with interesting cords, but without skirts. Three distinct cord structures are used here – the four-strand, cabled suspension cord; the jute twine rolled around the mould; and the fine cotton twines used for the striping. The ball at the bottom is covered in a warp of deep yellow and ebony, and the tuft is made from the rest of the jute twine.

MATERIALS

■ 2 spools of Madeira Tanne cotton 30, in the following colours: dark ebony 792, deep yellow 760 and taupe 659

■ 200g (7oz) of fine jute

■ Mould, see page 155

■ Ballpoint pen

■ Indian ink and paintbrush

■ Strong-impact adhesive

■ Strong polyester thread

■ Standard equipment

Suspension cord: make a four-strand cord using four warps, each of 3m (3¼yd): one of 20 ends jute; one of 120 ends ebony and deep yellow cotton; one of 20 ends jute; one of 120 ends ebony and taupe cotton (see steps 1–3).

Mould: make a two-strand cord using two warps of 2 ends x 11m (12yd) of jute. Spin up each warp and ply together.

Striping: make three two-strand cords using two warps of 4 ends x 1.5m (1¾yd) in deep yellow, and one each of 4 ends x 3m (3¼yd) in taupe and ebony. Spin the deep yellow and taupe cords Z and ply S, and spin the ebony cord S and ply Z. Cut the ebony and taupe in half.

Ball: make a warp of 20 ends x 1m (39in) using deep yellow and ebony cotton mixed.

1 Take each warp, loop it over the post and onto the cabler. Z spin. The first spin should not be too tight. S ply together. Knot the ends.

2 When all the twines have been spun, loop them all back onto the cabler and continue to spin S tightly.

3 Then Z ply all of the twines together. Bind the ends to prevent them unravelling.

4 Mark the mould, just to one side of centre. Paint the larger half with four coats of Indian ink to give a surface like ebony.

5 Roll round the mould from the painted area to the top with a long jute twine. Glue liberally, a couple of centimetres (1in) at a time, then wind the twine on top.

6 Wind the striping cords round the warping post in a figure-of-eight, following the colour sequence shown. Take the stripes over the mould using the technique for covering a mould.

7 Hook the binding yarn over the stripes and down through the mould. Turn the mould round 75° for the second stripe.

8 Lay the stripes at 75°
angles. On the last stripe,
finish off with two half-hitches
(see page 44).

9 Wrap some ebony cotton
round the mould to keep
the striping in place. Stitch a
cross, then take the yarn round
to the next stripe, underneath
the jute.

10 Bind a strong thread to
the suspension cord and
take it through the mould.

11 Cover the ball then take
the thread through and
secure very tightly round a tuft
of jute twine.

Moulds & Skirts

This chapter explores the design possibilities of tassel moulds and skirts, and how to balance them in colour, proportion and decoration. It shows the diverse shapes of moulds that you can buy and also the range of other materials that can be substituted for traditional moulds such as curtain finials or rolled paper shapes.

Left: These classical designs of tie-backs and small tassels are a good example of how diverse the shape of wooden tassel moulds can be. The tassels are made from silk and the moulds are made from gilded wood, with cut skirts.

Introduction

As we saw on pages 43 and 44, there are two basic ways of treating a tassel mould – covering and rolling. To roll a mould, use a strong-impact adhesive that does not dry too quickly and wind a gimp or cord around the mould in a spiral, from top to bottom. To cover a mould a warp is made, long enough to cover the outside of the mould back and forth, and is laced by a strong single thread on the inside. All kinds of embellishments can be worked on top, including striping, snailing and netting.

To space and spread the skirt evenly round the tassel mould, a technique of wiring the skirt warp over a board was developed. On old, dilapidated tassels – very useful for understanding tassel construction – the skirts are often woven and you can still see the narrow warp that forms the heading underneath the ruff. The later technique of twining the skirt warp with fine wire meant that the tassel maker could work independently from

Above: Multiple tassel moulds create elegant tassels. These cut skirts have been bound at the bottom, and are neatly cropped to give a good pompom edge.

the weaver, each at his or her own pace in the workshop. There are two basic skirt types – a cut skirt and a bullion skirt. Both can be decorated in many different ways, using tufts, drops, pompoms, jasmins, over-bullions and trellising.

Turned wooden moulds are used professionally for tassel tops, but you can create your own homemade moulds with rolled paper, glued squares of card or

Above: This African-style tassel with its painted and covered mould and rafia skirt, and this large pendant tassel, both show exciting combinations of skirts and moulds.

papier-mâché. You can also use finials from the ends of curtain poles or wooden beads. When decorating moulds do not feel confined to covering them with threads. You can paint or decorate them with découpage or papier-mâché.

Fine cotton, wool, rayon or polyester thread, and rayon gimp are suitable for the tassel skirt. They all hang well and swing when the tassel moves.

Opposite: These striking tassels are made of a series of covered moulds in strong, plain colours. They take their origins from Japanese designs.

Left: Today tassel moulds are normally turned in wood, but this Afghani beaded tassel is formed round stuffed fabric.

Finial Tassel

*C*urtain pole finials make excellent tassel moulds. This one was found in a box of odds and ends in a junkshop, and has had a 1.5cm (⅝in) hole drilled through it to take a reasonable-sized cord. The finial must have a hollowed bottom, in order to take the skirt – about 1cm (½in) minimum. Indigo blue linen yarns were used for the plain three-strand cord and skirt, to complement the finial's simple shape and stained surface.

The linen has quite a twist to it, and it needs to be steamed when the tassel is completed, and then combed out to get it to fall straight. Don't worry if it still spirals up – keep steaming and combing, and eventually the skirt will hang beautifully.

MATERIALS

- 1 spool of Borg's 16/2's linen, in light blue 596 and dark blue 296
- 1.2m (1¼yd) of 0.37mm (0.014in) galvanized wire
- 20cm (7¾in) of 1mm (0.04in) galvanized wire
- Wooden curtain pole finial
- Strong polyester thread
- Strong-impact adhesive
- Button
- Standard equipment

Suspension cord: make a three-strand cord using three warps of 38 ends x 1m (39in) in light blue, dark blue, and one mixed.

Skirt: make a warp of 32 ends x 15.5m (17yd), using both shades of blue and a 17cm (6¾in) skirt board.

1 Place a loop of 1mm (0.04in) wire through the cord and bind tightly.

2 Pass the wire through the centre of the mould. Wind the skirt round the wire.

3 Fit the skirt into the finial to see whether you have enough tags.

4 Make the appropriate adjustments, either adding or removing a few tags. Twist the wires together.

5 Stitch through the skirt using polyester thread.

6 Thread a button onto the wires, then glue the top of the skirt and twist up the wires tightly, using round-nosed pliers.

7 Knot the cord by making a single loop and threading the rest of the cord through it. Cut and trim the skirt, then steam well.

Loop Skirt Tassel

MATERIALS

- 1 x 4m (4⅓yd) packet of white gimp

- 2 x 4m (4⅓yd) packet of straw yellow gimp

- 1 spool of Madeira Tanne cotton 30, in three colours: green 711, yellow 610 and white 752

- Mould, see page 154

- Reusable adhesive

- Strong-impact adhesive

- Strong polyester thread

- Standard equipment

The skirt of this pretty tassel is made by simply winding yarn into loops and gathering them on a string. Each loop is hung with a tuft, which bulks it out nicely. Wind the same amount of yarn for the tufts as for the loops, so that when the tufts are folded over the loops and bound you have exactly double the quantity of ends. In general, this proportion produces a nicely weighted skirt

Roll the mould carefully, making sure that the gimp goes on level. Be economical with the glue, even if this means that it dries quickly and you have to re-glue as you make your way down the mould. The gimp is quite fine and the glue will seep through and stain it if it is too thick.

Suspension cord: make a three-strand cord using three warps of 3 ends of white gimp, 3 ends of yellow gimp, and 20 ends of green cotton yarn, all 1.1m (1¼yd) long. Ply them together, then make the cord into a loop and knot the ends together.

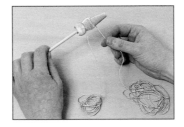

1 Place a knitting needle inside the mould and secure with a little reusable adhesive. Glue the mould and roll the yellow gimp on evenly.

2 On a 5cm (2in) board, wind the green yarn round 60 times at a slight angle so that it will slip off easily. On a 10cm (4in) board, wind the yellow yarn 60 times.

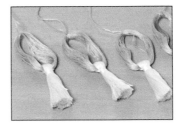

3 Tie the ends together to finish the loops. Slip a yellow loop through a green loop, and bind with white. Hide the knots in the binding. Make nine tassels in this way.

4 Knot the ends of the suspension cord. Take the cord through the mould. Tie the loops onto the cord.

5 Pad the tassel out by winding white yarn round a 12cm (4¾in) board 500 times. Lay the white yarn over the cord, as shown.

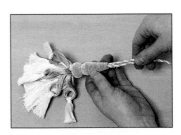

6 Pull the whole tassel up into the mould, and apply a generous dab of glue to hold it in place.

Copper Tassel

The decorative panel used on the mould for this tassel is a piece of thin copper sheeting from a car radiator, found in a scrap-merchant's yard. Necessity is the mother of invention! If you cannot find a similar piece of copper, substitute some wrapped yarn or very thin plain copper sheeting instead. Alternatively, you can mark the mould to give the same effect. The copper has been varnished, which sets off the pink rayon yarn beautifully.

The mould itself is made of rolled paper. Once you have mastered this technique, you can invent new shapes for your own tassels.

MATERIALS

- 100g (4oz) of William Hall's 1200/2's rayon, in pink

- 1.2m (1¼yd) of 0.37mm (0.014in) galvanized wire

- A1 sheet of good-quality cartridge paper

- Metal ruler

- Craft knife and board

- 1cm (½in) diameter wooden dowel

- PVA glue, diluted with a little water, and spreader

- Brown ink and paintbrush

- Woodstain

- Piece of thin copper sheeting

- Clear varnish and brush

- Standard equipment

Suspension cord: make a two-strand cord using two warps of 30 ends x 2.7m (3yd).

Skirt: make a warp of 24 ends x 22m (24yd) using a 21cm (8½in) board.

1 Mark the cartridge paper into strips lengthways, and cut two strips x 11cm (4½in), three strips x 8.5cm (3½in), two strips x 4cm (1½in), two strips x 1cm (½in) and four strips x 5mm (¼in).

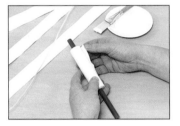

2 Using the dowel, start to roll the first set of papers. After 3cm (1¼in), start to glue so that the roll of paper does not stick to the dowel.

3 Measure 5mm (¼in) down from the top and roll the next set of papers. Measure 2.5cm (1in) down again, then roll the next set of papers.

4 Wrap the 1cm (½in) strips on the base, then finish with the fine strips.

5 Paint the paper mould with brown ink. It should look patchy. Next apply a layer of woodstain to get a deep, rich colour.

6 Glue the copper strip round the centre of the mould. Varnish the whole of the mould and leave to dry. Wind pink yarn to decorate the narrow parts of the mould.

7 Pass the ends of the suspension cord through the mould. Then wind the skirt around the mould. Steam and trim the skirt.

Découpage Tassel

Découpage, a favourite Victorian technique, is used here to decorate a large wooden bead and make an original mould. Cut motifs out of wrapping paper or magazines and stick them on with glue – the technique is so simple, and so decorative. The bead is painted with black acrylic paint, but you can experiment with different coloured backgrounds to fit in with your colour scheme.

A sink plug is attached to the bottom of the suspension cord and this holds the skirt out. This tip is very useful whenever you want to improvise with an unusual found object and turn it into a tassel mould.

MATERIALS

- 1 spool of Madeira Tanne cotton 30, in each of the following colours: pale pink 590, pink 592, pale mauve 639 and salmon pink 700

- 1.2m (1¼yd) of 0.37mm (0.014in) galvanized wire

- Large wooden barrel bead

- Pen or pencil

- Sandpaper

- White emulsion paint, and paintbrush

- Black acrylic paint

- Wrapping paper

- PVA glue and spreader

- Clear varnish and brush

- 4cm (1½in) sink plug

- Craft knife

- Standard equipment

Suspension cord: make a four-strand cord using four warps of 96 ends x 1m (39in) in all four shades of yarn.

Skirt: make a chunky warp of 96 ends x 20m (21⅓yd), using all four shades of yarn and a 13cm (5¼in) skirt board.

1 Wedge the bead on the end of a pen. Sand it, then prime with white emulsion paint. Leave to dry, then paint with black acrylic paint. Put the pen in a jar of sand and leave the bead to dry.

2 Cut the shapes you wish to use out of the wrapping paper. You can use single motifs or a repeat pattern.

3 Glue the paper shapes onto the bead, being careful to position them neatly. Leave to dry.

4 Give the bead up to ten coats of varnish. Sand down the last two coats before the final coat to give a clear, smooth finish.

5 Enlarge the hole in the sink plug with a craft knife. Loop the cord in half, knot the ends, and thread it through the plug and the bead.

6 Wrap the skirt tightly round the cord. Pull up the cord, taking the skirt onto the bead. Trim the skirt.

7 Tie the cord in a knot just above the bead to secure.

Indigo Drop Tassel

This tassel is unusual because it does not have a skirt, but even so it has a lovely shape, and hangs beautifully. Suspend it in a window, or from a key to an antique bureau or mahogany corner cupboard. It is quite simple to make.

The cords on the top mould have been alternately S and Z spun, and then laid onto the mould together using the same covering technique as the bottom mould, which gives an interesting chevron effect. This technique is called "striping".

Suspension cord: make a two-strand cord using two warps, one of 20 ends x 1m (39in) in blue cotton and one of 2 strands x 1m (39in) in gimp.

Bottom mould: make warps of 20 ends x 4m (4¼yd) in each colour.

Striping: make fine two-strand cords, one using two warps of 4 ends x 1.7m (2yd) in buff cotton and cream cotton each. S spin and Z ply together, then cut in half and bind. Make another cord using two warps of 8 ends x 90cm (35½in). Z spin and S ply together.

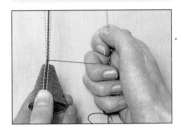

1 Roll the top mould with gimp. Figure-of-eight the three fine cords for the striping around the posts. Lay the cords down over the mould at 90° angles, beginning and ending the striping at the bottom.

2 Divide the bottom mould into eight equal sections, and cover them in cream and buff yarn.

3 Bind the bottom mould three times round with polyester thread to scoop in the shape.

4 Then replace this with a deeper binding in blue cotton. Snip off the polyester thread carefully.

5 Stitch the end of the blue binding thread securely into the covering.

6 Loop and bind the suspension cord, then pull it through the tassel. Make the tuft at the bottom by winding the blue cotton round your fingers 50 times, then binding and cutting it. Glue in place.

Peg Top Tassel

These charming tassels are rolled with two different coloured gimps to give a striped effect, and they have a wired skirt tucked inside the mould at the bottom. They are simple and quick to make as there is no elaboration.

Peg top tassels are small and light enough to be used on accessories, perhaps on a bag or hat. They could also be used, on a longer cord, to hang a painting or embroidery on the wall. Try contrasting colours for the mould and the skirt, with just one gimp rolled around the mould instead of two.

MATERIALS

- 1 spool of Madeira Tanne cotton 30, in yellow 772

- 1 x 4m (4¼yd) packet of gimp, in yellow and black

- 1.2m (1¼yd) of 0.37mm (0.014in) galvanized wire

- Mould, see page 155

- Reusable adhesive

- Strong-impact adhesive

- Standard equipment

Suspension cord: make a two-strand cord using two warps of 20 ends x 1m (39in) in yellow cotton.

Skirt: make a warp of 20 ends x 7.4m (8yd) over a 7.5cm (3in) board, using yellow cotton (see step 3).

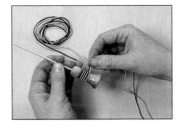

1 Place a knitting needle inside the mould and secure with a little reusable adhesive. Leaving 45cm (18in) free at the beginning, glue and roll the gimps round the mould from the neck down.

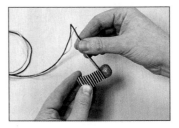

2 Take the needle out then glue and roll the top.

3 Make the skirt on a 7.5cm (3in) board. Be sure to make the skirt very neat and tight as the skirt wires must not show.

4 Take the suspension cord and knot the ends together. Pass through the mould. Wind the skirt round the cord.

5 Twist the skirt wires together.

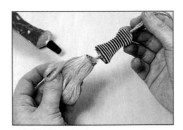

6 Glue the skirt top and pull it up into the mould. Leave to dry.

7 Cut the loops of the skirt and trim.

Tiny Pompom Tassel

This colourful little tassel is perfect for using up yarns left over from other projects. It is a good idea to prepare three or four spools of each colour as you need to wind an enormous quantity for a really full pompom. Take time to trim it well, and make sure that you bind the middle of the tassel very tightly to prevent any yarns from escaping. Small tassels like this one make delightful presents.

Suspension cord: make a two-strand cord using two warps of 20 ends x 1.1m (42in), in red cotton yarn. Knot or bind the ends securely before they unravel.

1 Wind the yarns in sequence round a 7cm (2¾in) board – green 300 times, red 30 times, blue 150 times, lime 150 times, yellow 250 times and violet 150 times.

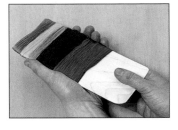

2 Carefully slip the yarn off the board, keeping the yarns in sequence.

3 Bind securely round the middle. Make sure you knot the binding very tightly otherwise threads will pull out of the pompom.

4 Cut through the loops and trim the tassel well with sharp scissors.

5 Form the tassel into a ball, still trimming and shaping.

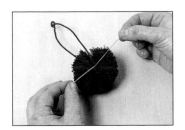

6 Tie the pompom securely onto the suspension cord with strong polyester thread.

7 Cover the tassel mould with 20 ends x 1m (39in) of lime yarn. Bind with red yarn. Thread the suspension cord through and knot it to keep the mould in place.

Snailed Tassel

Snailing is a technique of crossing the mould with cords. It looks best on a mould with a rounded shape so that the snailing stays in place. When the snailing is completed, the cords are placed over and under each other alternately, all the way round the mould, to form a four-point star when seen from above. Use S and Z spun cords to give a chevron effect. The main part of the skirt is cotton, with gold yarn used sparingly for the top layer. Metallic yarns are very light so the cotton is needed to give the skirt weight.

MATERIALS

- 1 spool of Madeira Tanne cotton 30, in taupe 36

- 1 reel of Madeira Gold 6 FS 5/2, No. 4, and 1 spool each of metallic yarns FS 2/2, No. 20, in shades 424, 425 and 426

- 1 x 4m (4⅜yd) packet of taupe gimp

- 1.2m (1⅜yd) of 0.37mm (0.014in) galvanized wire

- Mould, see page 153

- Strong-impact adhesive

- Strong polyester thread

- Standard equipment

Suspension cord: make a three-strand cord using one warp of 36 ends 1.2m (1⅜yd) in taupe yarn and 36 ends x 1.2m (1⅜yd) in metallic yarns. S spin and Z ply but put a lot of overtwist on the ply so spin up tightly. Then make a warp of 74 ends x 1.1m (42in) in taupe yarn, Z ply this warp, then S ply the two together. Bind the ends.

Binding: make a two-strand cord using two warps of 8 ends x 1m (39in) using the metallic yarns.

Gold snailing: make a two-strand cord using two warps of 8 ends x 75cm (30in), using all the metallic yarns. S twist and Z ply.

Taupe snailing cords: make a two-strand cord using two warps of 8 ends x 80cm (32in) of taupe gimp. Z twist and S ply.

Skirt: make a warp in taupe cotton of 24 ends x 20m (21⅞yd) and another warp of 24 ends x 10.5m (11⅛yd), using all the metallic yarns. The skirt has 75 tags of taupe yarn and 35 tags of metallic yarns (see steps 10 and 11).

1 Roll the mould with the gimp, using the glue to attach it. As this shape is difficult to roll, start 1m (39in) down the gimp and at the neck of the mould, then complete the top.

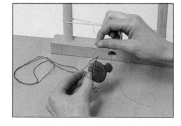

2 Bind the gold snailing cord to the waist of the mould with strong polyester thread.

3 Take the cord over and round the mould, so that it crosses over itself (see diagram overleaf).

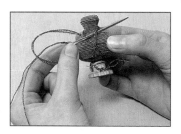

4 Take the cord round the mould again, *over* the next cord and then *under*. Go over at the bottom (see diagram overleaf).

Continued overleaf

5 Take the cord round a third time, going *under*, *over*, *over*, *under*. Go over at the bottom (see diagram).

6 Take the cord round the last time, going *over*, *under*, *over*, *under*, *over*, *under* the cords in sequence. Go over at the bottom (see diagram).

7 Make slight adjustments, shifting the cords carefully into place.

8 Looking at the mould from above, make a four-point star. Bind round the waist (see diagram).

9 Using the taupe cord, follow the previous snailing pattern, placing it between the other cords.

10 Make the warps for the skirt and make a skirt of 75 tags of taupe yarn and 35 tags of metallic yarns on a 13cm (5¼in) board.

11 Wrap the skirt round the mould three times with the metallic yarns as the outside row. Bind the waist of the tassel with a small amount of spare yarn.

12 Add the binding and stitch in place. Thread the cord through the tassel.

Below: A tassel tie-back decorated with snailing.

Papier-mâché Tassel

Papier-mâché is often used here as a medium for making tribal-looking heads and masks. Perhaps we can only just call this a tassel but it does hang, and it does have a head, a yarn skirt and a suspension cord. Allow the paper pulp to dry naturally for up to a week.

MATERIALS

- 40m (43¾yd) of natural jute twine, available from a hardware store or garden centre

- William Hall's 16/2's linen, in pale orange 1023

- 8 double sheets of newspaper

- Saucepan, electric blender and sieve

- 1 tbsp linseed oil

- A few drops of clove oil

- PVA glue and spreader

- 2 tbsp talcum powder

- 2 tbsp wallpaper paste

- Pencil and ruler

- Craft knife

- Sponge

- Copper enamel paint

- Green and black acrylic paint

- A4 sheet of cartridge paper

- Cocktail sticks

- Blue-green ink and brush

- 4m (4¼yd) strong polyester thread

- Strong-impact adhesive

- 240 x 2mm (⅛in) natural wooden beads

- 8 x 2mm (⅛in) brown beads

- Standard equipment

Suspension cord: make a two-strand cord using two warps of 2 ends x 60cm (24in) in jute. Spin up with a string of beads in one of the strands (see step 10).

Orange tassel: make a warp of 100 ends x 48cm (19in) in orange linen. Fold the warp in half and bind near the top. Cut the loops and add a suspension twine.

1 Tear the newspaper into small pieces, and soak in water overnight. Boil in plenty of water for 20 minutes. Strain and rinse thoroughly, to remove some of the newsprint.

2 Blend the paper in small batches, using plenty of water. Strain, leaving just enough water to give a soft lump that holds its shape. Mix in the linseed oil, clove oil, PVA glue, talcum powder and wallpaper paste thoroughly with your hands. Seal the pulp in a container.

3 Draw two paper templates to the shape of your mask. For the back, spread the pulp smoothly about 8mm (⅜in) thick. The front should be 4cm (1½in) thick at the thickest point (eyebrows), and 2cm (¾in) at the thinnest (chin). The pulp will shrink as it dries.

4 Sponge the mould with copper paint, and leave to dry. Sponge the mould with green acrylic paint, dry, then sponge again with a mixture of copper and black acrylic paint.

5 To make the beads, cut the cartridge paper as follows: one strip 5cm (2in) long x 2cm (¾in) wide, two strips 5cm (2in) long x 1cm (½in) wide and 15 x 5cm (2in) squares. Roll the strips round a cocktail stick and secure with PVA glue.

6 When the glue is dry, paint the beads with bright blue-green ink, then sponge them with copper paint.

Continued overleaf

7 With sharp scissors, cut eight of the 15 beads made from the paper squares into six equal pieces each. Cut each of the remaining seven of these beads into 12 equal pieces.

8 Pierce all the beads lengthways or across the centre, using a sharp sewing needle.

9 String the paper beads and the wooden beads onto the polyester thread to make several necklaces.

10 Spin up the cord. Make two more cords in exactly the same way but without the beads.

11 Bind and glue the cords to the back of the mask as shown, adding decoration as required. Glue the necklaces and the orange tassel in place.

12 For the hair, glue on four jute tassels, which hang down below the orange tassel. Trim all the tassels.

Left: Two examples of tassels made by contemporary designers. Like the African mask opposite, the tassel in the right of this picture, which has a beaded raffia skirt, is based on an African theme.

Spiral Tassel

*T*his is a very cheap and ingenious way to make your own mould. Tassels are mostly designed in the round but this one has a flattened shape, which makes an interesting change. When you are cutting the card into squares, use a cutting mat (available from good art shops) or a second piece of card underneath the mounting card, so that you do not mark the table top or work surface. Also use a wide, heavy metal ruler. The skirt is simply knotted onto the cord and looped round the mould. The long cord is formed into a double loop, so the tassel makes a curtain tie-back. The card for this mould has been cut into squares. Alternatively, you could make a very effective mould by cutting circular discs of different sizes instead. For an interesting angular-shaped mould you could cut the cord in diamond or triangular shapes.

Suspension cord: make a two-strand cord using two warps of 30 ends x 3m (3¼yd).

String of tassels: make 12 warps of 100 ends x 23cm (9in).

1 Cut four pieces of card 6.5 x 6.5cm (2½ x 2½in). Reducing the measurements 5mm (¼in) each time, cut 11 more pairs of squares. The last pair of squares should be 1 x 1cm (½ x ½in).

2 Squeeze enough blue paint for all the pieces of card and paint the smallest squares. Add a little black paint each time you paint a pair of squares, so that the largest squares are the darkest blue. Leave to dry.

3 Glue two of the largest squares together. Take one square of each size and glue together to form a spiral. Repeat to form a second spiral. Dip your finger in the gold ink and touch up the corners of the squares.

4 Cut four pieces of card 4.5 x 4.5cm (1¾ x 1¾in) square, glue together and paint. Glue to the centre of one spiral for the back of the mould, then glue on the other spiral for the front.

5 Knot the cord about 41cm (16½ in) from the ends, to make a loop. Halve that loop, and bind tightly.

6 Fold each warp for the tassels over the cord and bind. There should be six on either side, 6cm (2⅜in) from the central binding.

7 Take the cord round the mould, and bind it together at the bottom.

8 Unravel the cord in the centre, and steam and comb it out. Cut the fringe to a good point, following the line of the diamond shape of the mould.

Feathered Tassel

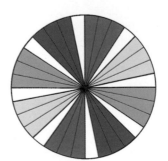

Diagram

*T*his tassel is inspired by the art of the Ndebele people of the Transvaal in South Africa. It is decorated with clear primary and secondary colours, plus shades and tints. The geometric blocks are outlined in black and white, which enhances the cool, hard-edged design. The moulds are made of cartridge paper and the skill here is to get even colour spacings.

Suspension cord: make a two-strand cord using two warps of 30 ends x 2m (2¼yd) in black linen.

Mould: make warps of 24 ends x 2.5m (2¾yd) in black and white cotton, and 1.5m (1¾yd) in each of the other colours.

Black skirt: make a warp of 22 ends x 20m (21¾yd) each of rayon and cotton, using a 23cm (9in) skirt board.

Paper moulds: cut the cartridge paper lengthways into strips, as follows: 23 strips x 1.25cm (⁹⁄₁₆in), 17 strips x 4cm (1½in) 8 strips x 1.5cm (⅝in). Roll up and glue the strips over the dowel, until you have the following measurements: two 1.25cm (⁹⁄₁₆in) wide x 2cm (¾in) diameter, two 1.25cm (⁹⁄₁₆in) wide x 4.5cm (1¾in) diameter, one 1.5cm (⅝in) wide x 4.5cm (1¾in) diameter,

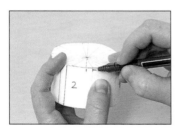

1 Using the diagram as a guide, mark the radiating lines on the mould.

2 Sand down the moulds to get rid of the rough edges of paper.

3 Cover the moulds, starting and finishing each colour separately (see diagram). Glue the moulds together.

4 To make the top skirt, wire the feathers together.

5 Attach the cord to a small circle of card, and pass it through the moulds. Glue the black skirt to the card, using the clear glue.

6 Wind the feather skirt on top of the black skirt. Pull up the cord and secure.

Panelled Skirt Tassel

O*n this dramatic tassel the skirt goes round the tassel mould twice. The first row is a mixture of the chestnut brown and blue yarn, and the second row is equal panels of chestnut brown and then blue. If you are very clever, you could make the ruffs and the covering of the mould do the same, so that the tassel is a different colour on all four sides.*

It is a good idea to make a plain-colour tassel first so that you know exactly how many tags you need for the skirt, and how many loops for the ruffs. You can then divide them equally for the different colours.

Suspension cord: make a two-strand cord using two warps of 20 ends x 60cm (24in), one in blue and one in red.

Mould: make a warp of 20 ends x 1.1m (42in) in blue. Cover the mould then bind with strong polyester thread.

Skirt: on a 7.5cm (3in) board, make a warp of 20 ends x 4.5m (5yd), using both colours

– this is to go round the tassel mould exactly once. Make two warps of 2.6m (2⅞yd) in brown and blue separately for the second row of 32 tags, which is split equally into eight tags of each colour (see steps 1 and 2).

Ruffs: make warps from 20 ends x 1m (39in) of each colour, over a 2mm knitting needle.

1 Check that the first row of the skirt has the correct number of tags – it is better to over-estimate as it is easy to take off a few tags at the beginning of the skirt.

2 The second row must also fit the mould exactly. Twist the wires together to secure.

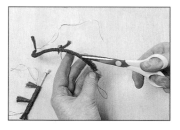

3 The bottom ruff is made with 27 loops of brown, and then 33 loops of blue. Cut through the loops with small, sharp scissors. The top ruff is made with nine loops of blue and 13 loops of brown.

4 Knot the ends of the suspension cords together. Take the cord through the tassel using a long needle and strong polyester thread looped around the cord. Attach the middle ruff by winding it around the join from top to bottom. Attach the top ruff to the cord. Trim the ruffs.

Wool Tassel with Pompoms

*W*ool is a beautifully easy material to use for tassels. Because it is bulky it is ideal for making larger tassels, but it is very light compared to other fibres so some thickness or extra yarn is necessary to give the tassel weight. In this tassel, the skirt is left uncut and a chunky pompom is attached to each pair of tags to bulk out the skirt and give it weight. When you are making the skirt, be careful not to twist the yellow warp as you wind it round the skirt board, so that the tags sit straight. The velvet quality of the cut ruffs matches the texture of the pompoms.

MATERIALS

- Appleton's crewel embroidery wool, in 25g (1oz) hanks: 1 red 866, 3 blue 925, 1 yellow 311 and 1 olive green 314

- Mould, see page 154

- Reusable adhesive

- 1.2m (1¼yd) of 0.37mm (0.014in) galvanized wire

- 3.25mm knitting needle

- Strong-impact adhesive

- Strong polyester thread

- Standard equipment

Suspension cord: make a four-strand cable cord using four warps of 15 ends x 3.5m (3⅞yd), one in red, one blue and two yellow. Spin up the red and blue warps and ply them together. Spin up the yellow warps and ply them together. Knot or bind the ends with strong polyester thread.

Mould: make a two-strand cord using two warps of 4 ends x 3.4m (3½yd) in red.

Skirt: make a warp of 20 ends x 10m (11yd) in yellow wool.

Ruffs: make a warp of 4m (4¼yd) x 20 ends, in olive green wool, over a 3.25mm knitting needle (see step 6).

1 Loop both strands over the post and onto the cabler. Twist up S and ply the four strands together Z. Use needles to keep the sequence.

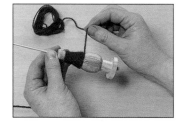

2 Leaving 60cm (24in) at the beginning, roll the mould with the red twine from the neck down. Finish by gluing and rolling the top.

3 Suspend two hanks of blue wool between the posts. Bind tightly at 1.5cm (⅝in) intervals, leaving 10cm (4in) of the binding yarn.

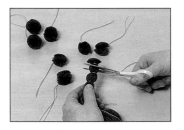

4 Cut halfway through each binding with sharp scissors. Fluff up the pompoms by rolling them between the palms of your hands.

5 Tie one pompom to every two tags of the skirt.

6 Make the ruffs longer than the needle. Work from the head end of the needle. The main ruff has 75 loops and the top ruff has 25.

7 Cut through both ruffs with small, sharp scissors. Take the cord through the mould and secure. Wind the skirt round the cord.

8 Bind the middle of the tassel with red wool so that the main ruff sits on a level base. Secure the ruffs on to the tassel.

Dip-dyed Silk Tassel

Dip-dyeing the yarn before you make a tassel gives exciting results. In the technique used here, the colours appear randomly throughout the tassel. You can use any hot or cold water dyes suitable for silk, following the instructions on the packet.

A niddy-noddy helps wind even skeins. It is commonly used to wind the spun wool off the spinning wheel bobbin, ready for scouring. Instead of a niddy-noddy, you can simply wind the warp round any object that gives an even skein, such as a large book.

MATERIALS

- 1 cone of Texere 2/27's silk, SS30
- Niddy-noddy
- Strong polyester thread
- Green and red dye
- Saucepan
- Mould, see page 154
- 1.2m, (1¼yd) of 0.37mm (0.014in) galvanized wire
- Standard equipment

1 Wind a small skein of silk yarn onto the niddy-noddy, or round a large book.

2 Tie the beginning and end threads together securely round the skein.

3 Attach four threads to keep the skein from tangling during the dyeing process.

4 Make a warp of 20 ends x 21m (23yd). Wind it onto the niddy-noddy and attach four threads. Tie the skeins together and scour in a hand-hot, soapy bath for 10 minutes. Then rinse.

5 Dissolve the green dye in water. Fold the skeins in half, then suspend them over the saucepan so that half the skein is submerged. Leave for about half an hour.

6 Dissolve the red dye in the same way. Rinse the skeins in hot water, turn them round and dye the other half in the red dye, so that the red "bleeds" into the green about 2cm (⅜in).

7 Rinse the yarns. Open out the skeins and pull them back into shape, then hang to dry. Wind the skeins into balls. Cut 1.5m (1⅔yd) off the thicker skein and cover the mould.

8 Using the thicker skein, make a skirt of 47 tags, on a 7cm (2¾in) board. Cut 1.5m (1⅔yd) off the warp and make a two-strand cord. Fold the remainder into four and make the tufts.

9 Using the thinner skein, bind the top of the tassel mould, then wind the skirt round the mould and secure. Bind over the join and trim the skirt. Attach the cord.

Woven Mould Tassel

Tassel moulds that have been covered and then stitched round are called "woven", presumably because the covering is vertical and the stitching horizontal, as in weaving. It is a technique that has been practised for centuries, and is intricate, skilful work which requires time and patience. Consequently, it is rarely used on modern tassels and is found more frequently on tassels from the 17th and 18th centuries. In this tassel, the trick is to section the tassel mould correctly so that the pattern fits the circular mould, forming an exact repeat.

MATERIALS

- Madeira Tanne cotton 30, in the following colours: 1 spool of green 577, 1 spool of yellow 760 and 2 spools of black 500

- 2.2m (2½yd) of 0.37mm (0.014in) galvanized wire

- 1 sheet of A1 good-quality cartridge paper

- PVA glue, diluted with a little water, and spreader

- 1cm (½in) diameter wooden dowel

- Sandpaper

- Clear glue

- Small circle of mounting board

- Standard equipment

Suspension cord: make a two-strand cord of 24 ends x 50cm (20in) in black cotton.

Mould: make warps of 24 ends x 3m (3¼yd) in green and in yellow, and a warp of 20 ends x 2.5m (2¾yd) in black.

Main skirt: make two warps – one of 12 ends x 20m (21¾yd) each of green and yellow cotton, and another of 24 ends x 5m (5½yd) in black. Wind the warps onto a 22.5cm (8⅞in) board in the following sequence: 4 tags green, 4 tags yellow and 1 tag black.

Top skirt: use a 10cm (4in) skirt board, with a warp of 24 ends x 9m (9¾yd) in black.

Paper moulds: cut the cartridge paper into strips: 16 strips x 1.25cm (⁹⁄₁₆in), 6 strips x 1.5cm (⅝in) and 13 strips x 5cm (2in). Make up the following moulds by rolling and gluing the strips with PVA glue over a 1cm (½in) dowel, until you reach the required diameter: two x 1.25cm (⁹⁄₁₆in) thick x 2.5cm (1in) diameter, three x 5cm (2in) thick x 2cm (¾in) diameter, two x 1.25cm (⁹⁄₁₆in) thick x 4.5cm (1¾in) diameter, two x 5cm (2in) thick x 6cm (2¼in) diameter and one x 1.5cm (⅝in) thick x 4.5cm (1¾in) diameter. Sand down the paper moulds to get rid of the rough edges.

1 Cover the paper moulds with the green, yellow and black warps. For the sectioned moulds, mark the moulds for the colour sequence following diagram 1, then cover.

2 For the weaving, mark the moulds following diagrams 2 and 3. (Each section marked on diagrams 2 and 3 is equal to one square in diagram 4). Take an even running stitch round the moulds with a marker thread, to use as a guide for the stitching. Stitch the pattern using 3 ends x 1m (39in) of black yarn. Follow diagram 4. Stitch three rows to give the correct depth for the pattern.

3 Using clear glue, attach the main skirt to the circle of mounting board. Thread the moulds onto the cord and glue together.

4 Fix the top skirt over the main skirt, and glue it to the circle of mounting board. Secure the cord and trim the tassel.

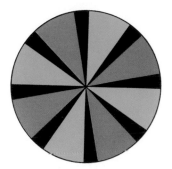

Diagram 1

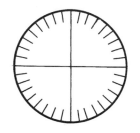

Diagram 2

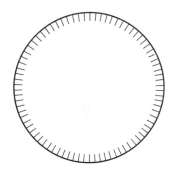

Diagram 3

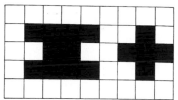

Diagram 4

$\mathscr{B}$ullions & $\mathscr{R}$uffs

$\mathbf{B}$ullion skirts and ruffs are the hallmark of a sophisticated tassel. Both of these techniques are complex and require practice to make perfect. The ruff must be entwined tightly with wire, and the bullion or warp laid evenly over the skirt board or needle to give a neat, compact finish. The techniques explained in this chapter can be applied to previous projects.

Left: These red and green silk tassels with bullion skirts, uncut ruffs and fan-edged braid were made for a set of silk curtains.

Introduction

Bullion is the name given to the technique of twisting up yarn so tightly that it spins back on itself as the skirt is being made to form a loop. The effect is to create an uncut loop skirt. This technique is found in the tassels made by the Central Asian nomads. Because of their lifestyle, any technique would require almost nothing in terms of equipment, and a bullion fringe is made by simply twisting up a few centimetres of yarn between the fingers and letting it ply back on itself. Nowadays, bullion twine is used to make tassels and fringes for fabrics and furnishings, and also for epaulettes on military uniforms and fringes on trade-union banners and flags.

Ruffs are used to increase the grandeur of a tassel and also to hide unsightly joins underneath, particularly where the cord joins the top of the tassel mould and where the skirt is wound round the waist. Ruffs also give emphasis to rosettes. The contemporary fashion is for small, tight ruffs, but antique tassels often have ruffs made of long loops of floss silk or ribbon, or fine spun twine. Cut ruffs give a luxurious velvet effect.

Above: Blue silk tassel with gold overbullions and a cut ruff. The cord was made using a Japanese braiding technique called *kumi-himo*.

Opposite: This tassel was specially commissioned to co-ordinate with a Fortuny fabric. It has gold detailing in the cord, a gimp-rolled mould, and a cut ruff and bullion skirt in toning shades.

Left: These silk tassels, which have single-strand bullion skirts, come from Afghanistan. The tassels on the right have a bead threaded onto the end of each bullion.

Tartan Drawstring Bag

*T*his is a charming little bag, with its tiny bullion tassels in the colours of the tartan fabric. The gimps are twisted up to form the bullions. Spin the gimp in the same direction as it was spun to create opposite twists. If you make the gimp the day before, the twist will deaden slightly and it will be easier to work; steam it to make the bullions twist up fully. Make the bullion skirts tight and crisp, so that the wires disappear into the mould. Make the cord loops first, then string them through the bag, adding the tassels last.

MATERIALS

- 1 spool of Madeira Tanne cotton 30, in each of the following colours: red 618, green 780, blue 583 and yellow 758

- 1 spool of Madeira Sticku 30, in white 1071

- Mould, see page 152

- Strong polyester thread

- 1.25cm (⅜in) diameter wooden dowel

- 4 x 4m (4¼yd) packets of red gimp

- 4 x 4m (4¼yd) packets of green gimp

- Bobbin

- Masking tape

- Strong-impact adhesive

- Standard equipment

Suspension cord: make a two-strand cord using two warps of 20 ends x 1.1m (42in) with one warp in red and one in green.

Mould: make a warp of 20 ends x 1.5m (1⅝yd) white Sticku.

Net: make a fine two-strand cord using two warps of 4 ends x 1.2m (1⅓yd) in blue cotton. Make the net following the method shown in steps 3-8 for the Linen Blind Pull on page 62.

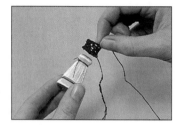

1 Cover the mould with the white Sticku, then bind with strong thread. Make one net on a 1.25cm (⅜in) dowel, eight loops round and four rows deep (see page 62 for method). Slip one net onto one of the tassel moulds. Then bind the mould with yellow cotton thread.

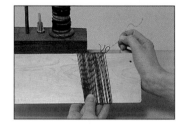

2 To make the bullions, twist the gimps, using a drill, until you have lost about 50cm (20in) in each of the 4m (4¼yd) lengths. Wind onto a bobbin and secure with masking tape. Make each skirt, using two red bullion twines followed by two green ones, on a 10cm (4in) board.

3 Make sure that you wind the bullions at the same angle, so that they will be an even length when they are taken off the board. Slip them off one by one, twisting each one as you go.

4 Steam the skirt over a boiling kettle to bring the twist back into the bullions.

5 Thread the cord through the mould. Knot the cord, then wind the skirt round it. Twist the wires together, glue the top of the skirt and pull it up into the mould.

Two-level Bullion Tassel

This unusual tassel has two skirts and an interesting cord. The wooden beads are optional, but they complement the design perfectly. Spin the mint green and yellow gimps ready to make the skirts and wind them onto a bobbin, taping down the ends so that they don't unravel. Leave them overnight for the twist to rest, and they will be quite easy to work with next day.

MATERIALS

- 4m (4¼yd) packets of gimp, in the following colours: 1 packet in indigo blue, 4 packets in mint green and 2 packets in yellow
- Bobbin
- Masking tape
- 1 spool of Madeira Tanne cotton 30, in yellow 759
- 2.5m (2⅜yd) of 0.37mm (0.014in) galvanized wire
- Mould, see page 153
- Reusable adhesive
- Strong-impact adhesive
- Clear glue
- 7 yellow beads
- Standard equipment

Suspension cord: make a three-strand cord using three warps: one of 2 ends x 1m (39in) indigo blue gimp; one of 2 ends x 1m (39in) mint green gimp; one of 20 ends x 1m (39in) yellow cotton. Z spin each warp then S ply together.

Yellow skirt: use 8m (8¾yd) of gimp and a 9cm (3⅝in) board. S twist the bullions one by one as you slip them off the board.

Mint green skirt: use 12m (13yd) of gimp and a 6cm (2¼in) board. S twist the bullions as you slip them off the board.

1 Roll the top part of the mould with indigo blue gimp, then thread the cord through – it is quite a tight fit. Steam the yellow skirt and wind it round the cord.

2 Pull the top of the skirt up into the mould. Twist the wires together with pliers to secure.

3 Steam the mint green skirt and wind it exactly twice round the mould, on top of the yellow skirt.

4 Twist the wires together tightly to secure, then bind the top of the skirt with yellow cotton.

5 Glue the beads at equal intervals round the mint green skirt.

Linen Tassel

*L*inen is an excellent yarn to use for a larger tassel. It holds its shape well and has body, and it stays neat and tidy. This tassel uses unbleached linen yarn, which has natural texture and makes the red linen look even more brilliant.

There's nothing extraordinary about the detailing on this tassel, it is just plain and handsome. The warps for the cord use a lot of ends, so they may take some time to make. Have a small length of knitting yarn or string ready to loop over the warps as you make them, so that you can count back easily every 20 or so ends.

MATERIALS

- 1 spool of Bocken's 16/1's linen, in red 1007 and unbleached linen

- 3.5m (3¾yd) of 0.37mm (0.014in) galvanised wire

- 20cm (7⅞in) of 1mm (0.04in) galvanised wire

- 3mm knitting needle

- Mould, see page 154

- Strong polyester thread

- Standard equipment

Suspension cord: make a three-strand cord using three warps of 120 ends x 1.5m (1⅝yd) with one warp in red, one in unbleached linen and one of red and unbleached linen mixed. Bind the ends.

Skirt: use the red and unbleached linen together to make a warp of 40 ends x 26.5m (29yd). Make the skirt on a 16cm (6½in) board, giving you 80 tags.

Ruffs: make a warp of 40 ends x 3.2m (3½yd) of red linen, using a 3mm needle and 1.2m (1¼yd) of wire for the bottom ruff, and 1m (39in) for the top ruff. The bottom ruff has 80 loops, and the top ruff 32.

Left: Natural fibres such as silk, linen or in this case cotton, show up particularly well when left undyed.

1 Cover the tassel mould with 24 ends x 2m (2⅛yd) of unbleached linen. Pass a loop of 1mm (0.04in) wire through the suspension cord and bind tightly. Take both ends of the wire through the mould and twist to secure.

2 Twist the skirt around the mould – it will go round the mould twice. Twist up the wires tightly to secure.

3 To finish, take the ruffs twice round the top of the skirt, with the longer ruff below the shorter one.

Tufted Tassel

As well as the normal skirt made on a board with wire, this tassel has an overskirt, with eight tufts suspended on a fine cord loop from the mould. This is a smart tassel to hang on a key from a bookcase or bureau.

MATERIALS

- 1 spool of Madeira Tanne cotton, 30, in red 622 and black 500

- 1 spool of Madeira Gold 6 F/S 5/2, 40

- 3.5m (3¾yd) of 0.37mm (0.014in) galvanized wire

- 2mm knitting needle

- Mould, see page 154

- Strong polyester thread

- 1.5cm (⅝in) diameter wooden dowel

- Clear glue

- Standard equipment

Suspension cord: make a two-strand cord using two warps of 20 ends x 1m (39in), one in red cotton and one in gold yarn.

Skirt: make a warp of 24 ends x 8m (8¾yd) on a 10cm (4in) board, using black cotton.

Overskirt: make two warps of 200 ends x 85cm (34in), in red, and red and black.

Fine cord: make a fine two-strand cord using two warps of 6 ends x 1.5m (1¾yd) in red cotton.

Ruff: make a warp of 40 ends x 1.8m (2⅛yd) of red cotton, using a 2mm knitting needle, and a 1.4m (1½yd) wire. You will need about 94 loops.

1 Cover the mould with a warp of 20 ends x 2.1m (2⅜yd) of gold yarn. Because of its conical shape, you will need to cram the warp at the top and spread it out at the bottom. Bind the middle.

2 Form the suspension cord into a loop and knot the ends together. Wind the skirt round the knot in the suspension cord.

3 Suspend the fine cord between two posts and loop one of the overskirt warps over it. The warp should hang down 10cm (4in) on either side of the cord. Take a double end of gold yarn and make a loop pointing to the bottom of the tuft. Bind tightly from top to bottom, then take the yarn through the loop at the bottom. Pull both ends so that the loop slips inside the binding. Cut the ends close. Bind all the red tufts onto the cord, then place the red-and-black tufts between them.

4 To make the overskirt, prepare a wire and wrap it round the fine cord, as if for an ordinary skirt. Take the cord round the front and up the back of the dowel, leaving a tuft suspended at the bottom. Make about six twists in the wire, and loop the cord again. Twist up and continue until all the tufts are completed.

5 Glue the top of the underskirt and pull it up into the mould.

6 Wrap the overskirt round the mould – it should go exactly once round. Secure the wires. Attach the ruff – it should go round the tassel mould three times.

Trellised Tassel

This tassel has a smart, trellised overskirt and a three-strand cabled cord. It shows how handsome a tassel can be made in only two colours. Two shades of red are used, very close to each other, which give more depth to the colour. The mould is rolled with gimp and the cord fits into a little cup, covered in red and black, which makes a neat way to hide the end of the cord. Be careful to bind at the same level on each trellis, and to comb the trellis strands so that they fall evenly.

MATERIALS

- Madeira Tanne cotton 30, in the following colours: 2 spools of black 500, 1 spool of scarlet 618 and 1 spool of brick red 622

- 3m (3¼yd) of red gimp

- 4m (4⅜yd) of 0.37mm (0.014in) galvanized wire

- Mould, see page 152

- Reusable adhesive

- Strong-impact adhesive

- Standard equipment

Suspension cord: make a three-strand cabled cord using three warps of 50 ends x 1.5m (1¾yd), with one warp in black, one warp in scarlet and brick red, and one warp which is one part scarlet, one part brick red and two parts black.

Underskirt: use 30 ends x 15m (16½yd) of black cotton and a 10cm (4in) board.

Ruff: make a warp of 40 ends x 1.7m (2yd) of both reds and black mixed. You will need about 115 loops. As it is quite long, 1.5m (1¾yd) of wire, folded to 75cm (30in).

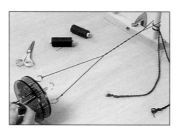

1 First roll the mould with gimp. Then twist up each of the warps for the cord quite lightly, one at a time, and ply back. Bind the ends.

2 Now twist up the plied strands until they are just about to kink up.

3 Then ply back the strands. Bind the ends together to prevent the cord unravelling.

4 For the trellised overskirt, make a warp of 100 ends x 2m (2¼yd), using all four spools. Loop them over a wire, twisting a little between each loop to get the overskirt to fit exactly round the underskirt (see page 114 for method).

5 First wind the underskirt round the mould and secure. Attach the overskirt over the black underskirt. Cut through the loops. Cover the small cup mould with a mixture of red and black cotton.

6 Comb out the ends of the overskirt. Bind the ends together, taking right over left in each pair to create the trellised effect. Finally, take the cord through the mould.

Tropical Fish Tassel

This tassel was inspired by studies of tropical fish. The fish's markings are depicted by gimps trailing over the mould, and the vivid tropical marine life is captured in the orange, turquoise and black colours. Slippery polyester yarns are used in the skirt to capture the watery sway as the tassel moves. The trellised overskirt is carefully placed between the gimp on the mould. A curtain ring is glued to the mould, providing a ledge for the skirt to sit on. The mould is a foot for a chest of drawers, available from any DIY store, with an 8mm (⅜in) hole drilled through the middle.

MATERIALS

- 12m (13yd) of turquoise gimp

- 12m (13yd) of black gimp

- 2 spools of Madeira Neon, in yellow 1925 and orange 1955

- 1 spool of Madeira Tanne cotton 30, in turquoise 649 and black 500

- 2.2m (2½yd) of 0.37mm (0.014in) galvanized wire

- Mould (see introduction), sanded and primed with emulsion paint

- Acrylic paint, in lemon yellow and vermilion

- Sponge

- Paper, pencil and ruler

- Clear glue

- Paintbrush

- Curtain ring

- Strong polyester thread

- Strong-impact adhesive

- 6.5mm knitting needle

- Circle of mounting card

- Standard equipment

Suspension cord: make a three-strand cord using three warps, one each of 6 ends x 1.4m (1½yd) in turquoise and black gimp, and one 100 ends x 1.4m (1½yd) in yellow and orange Neon mixed. Twist each strand S, then ply them all Z. Bind the ends tightly to secure.

Skirt: use the turquoise, black and orange yarns to make 72 ends x 15m (16½yd) over a 20cm (7¾in) board. It should go once round the mould.

1 Sponge the mould with lemon yellow paint. Mix some lemon yellow and vermilion paint and sponge over the yellow background while it is still wet.

2 Cut a piece of paper to fit round the mould, and divide it into seven sections. Mark the mould with straight lines down towards the base, and wavy lines up over the top.

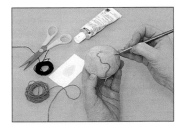

3 Glue the marked lines carefully with a paintbrush, so that you can control the spread of glue accurately. Lay on the turquoise gimp.

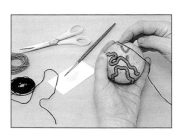

4 Stick another length of gimp round the central one, then outline with the black gimp.

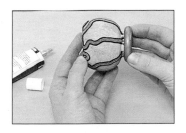

5 Glue the curtain ring to the bottom of the mould. Using a 25cm (10in) board, make 14 tassels in yellow and orange Neon, wrapping the yarns round the board 240 times. Slip each tassel off the board and bind with thread.

6 Tie another thread three-quarters down each tassel to keep them separated. Stitch the threads into the skirt in pairs, holding the skirt against the mould to check the tassels are placed in the spaces between the gimps.

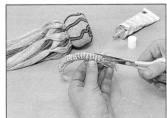

7 Attach the skirt. Trellis the tassels – in each pair, take right over left and bind to the next tassel.

8 Make a warp of 240 ends x 1m (39in), and make a ruff over a 6.5mm knitting needle and a 1.2m (1¼yd) wire. Glue the spine to the ruff. Leave to dry, then cut through the loops and attach to the tassel.

9 Knot the ends of the cord together. Thread the cord through the card circle and then through the tassel.

Shell Mosaic Tassel

Mosaic is a lovely way to decorate a tassel mould, and here the broken shells are particularly inventive. The result is very delicate. The texture of the crochet cotton sets off the shells beautifully. Only alternate loops in the ruff are cut, and this also adds to the textured effect. The mould is simply a doorknob from a hardware store. Choose shells of similar colouring and not too domed, so that they will stick onto the mould easily.

MATERIALS

- 1 x 50g (2oz) ball of no.20 crochet cotton, in mink 503 and off-white 502

- 1 x 20g (¾oz) ball of no.20 crochet cotton, in random-dyed mink

- 3.2m (3½yd) of 0.37mm (0.014in) galvanized wire

- About 12 shells of even thickness, broken

- 5cm (2in) diameter doorknob, with a 1cm (⅓in) hole drilled through the middle, primed with off-white emulsion paint

- Clear glue

- Clear varnish and brush

- 3mm knitting needle

- Strong polyester thread

- Standard equipment

Suspension cord: make a two-strand suspension cord using two warps of 18 ends x 75cm (30in) in mink and off-white.

Skirt: make 30 ends x 6m (6½yd) on a 10cm (4in) board, using all three colours of crochet cotton.

1 Lay the broken shell pieces on your work surface. Carefully glue the shell fragments onto the doorknob, making sure that the whole surface is covered. Apply a coat of varnish with a paintbrush and leave until completely dry.

2 Make the large ruff from 18 ends x 1m (39in) on a 3mm needle, using off-white and 1.2m (1¼yd) of wire. Make the small ruff from 9 ends x 50cm (20in), again using off-white and 75cm (30in) of wire.

3 Attach the skirt to the mould, then wind the larger ruff around the mould. Fix this in place too.

4 Knot the ends of the cord. Thread a needle with strong polyester thread and loop it around the suspension cord. Take the cord through the mould.

5 Attach the smaller ruff to the top of the mould where the cord comes out of the mould. Carefully cut the loops of the skirt and trim.

6 To finish off the tassel, cut every alternate loop of the large ruff with a pair of sharp scissors.

Bead Skirt Tassel

Covered beads are strung into drops for this tassel, making an unusual alternative to a cut or bullion yarn skirt. The result is almost like a piece of jewellery, and indeed the tassel could be worn as a brooch or hair ornament. Look out for beads that have a reasonably large central hole, as, of course, the holes fill up as you cover them. If you cannot find suitable beads, you can always drill larger holes with an electric drill, sandwiching each bead in a small vice. The flattened tufts between the beads add a velvet-like quality.

MATERIALS

- 1 spool of Madeira Tanne cotton 30, in grey 736, green 577 and red 618

- Mould, see page 154

- 24 small barrel beads

- Hammer

- 1.5m (1⅝yd) of 0.37mm (0.014in) galvanized wire

- 2mm knitting needle

- Standard equipment

Suspension cord: make a two-stranded cord using one warp of 20 ends x 1.2m (1¼yd) in grey. Loop the warp over the post, attach both ends to the cabler, then spin up.

Fine cord: two-stranded cord for stringing the beads using two warps of 4 ends x 1m (39in) each in grey.

Mould: cover with 20 ends x 1.1m (42in) of grey yarn.

Beads: cover the beads with warps of 20 ends x 50cm (20in) in each colour or colour-mixes. The top six beads are grey/green, the second row green, the third row red/grey, and the last row red.

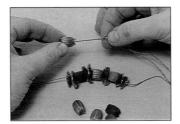

1 First make the tufts. Wind 300 ends x 50cm (20in) of grey yarn, and bind every 1.25cm (⅛in). Cut the warp between the ties, flatten out the tufts between your fingers, then hammer them to flatten them completely.

2 String the covered beads and tufts onto the fine cord, making a good knot at both ends of each string. Steam over a kettle to fluff up the tufts.

3 Bind the strings onto the tassel mould, so that the top beads hang just below the mould. Catch the knots just under the binding.

4 Make a ruff of 40 ends x 1.5m (1⅝yd) in red yarn, using a 2mm knitting needle. Wind round the tassel three times. Knot the ends of the suspension cord and attach it to the tassel.

Embellishments

This chapter focuses on the additional embellishments that can be incorporated into tassel design — different types of embrace for curtains, tassels for scarves, rosettes and Turk's head knots. Tassels are primarily associated with interior decoration, but the techniques can be adapted for dress and two projects are devoted to this.

Left: These extremely ornate double tassel tie-backs are entirely handmade. (Left) This tassel is part of a range called "Sultan" because the design shows Arabian influences. There is gimp detailing on the mould and a hand-crocheted skirt with tiny tassels hanging from it. (Right) The tiny tassels coming down the skirt are quite exquisite.

Introduction

Rosettes come in many forms, usually with a gimp trellis formation round the outside. They are used on cushions, particularly bolsters, and on pleated curtain valances and pelmets. The rosette and tassel in this chapter are of French origin, and are made in the traditional colours – pale indigo and soft madder pink – which are typical of French passementerie.

Tie-backs use a lot of yarn, so jute is a good choice for your first attempt – it is an inexpensive and easy fibre to use, and fits into most modern interiors. This is an opportunity to use silk, also – the most economical way to buy it is undyed

Right: Double tassel tie-back in rich olive-green and red, and good bulky tufted skirts in two layers.

Above: A 19th-century vellum rosette and tassel. The rosette is covered in fine monofilament silk.

Left: This silk tassel has a matching rosette. The silk has been dip-dyed so that the colour moves from green to black.

from a weavers' supplier. The design given here for an ecru silk double tassel tie-back is very elegant, and suits different interiors and fabrics. If you are on a tight budget, another way of using expensive threads without being too extravagant is to mix cheaper yarns in with expensive ones. Alternatively you can pad out the under part of the skirt and save the silk for the top layer.

Knots are one of the most satisfying forms of decoration on tassels. They can be used on the suspension cord, as a head for a tassel, or as an embellishment on the tassel itself. Some

knots work all three ways – the Turk's head knot, for instance, may encircle the holding cord, form the head of the tassel, or serve as a flat decoration. The Turk's head knot is shown in this chapter but the options for including other knots in tassel making are endless.

Scarves and shawls look especially well finished with the addition of an eye-catching tassel. The grey-and-black scarf with tassels is an elegant accessory for a plain black coat, and the Chinese tassel on a silk shawl is an unusual evening accessory which is guaranteed to make an impact at a ball or evening party.

Above: Rosette, tassel, woven braid and cord. These have been designed to be used together on a Victorian settee. The rosette and tassel are for the bolster, the braid covers the join between the upholstery and the wood surround, and the cord is for the seat cushions.

Tassel with Cut Ruff

This is a very elegant tassel which you can attach to an evening cloak or heavy silk wrap to give a grand Chinese effect. The proportions of oriental tassels are much longer than European ones, and they are found on fans, rolled documents and so on, rather than furnishings. This tassel is typical of the early 19th-century fashion for chinoiserie. It has a cut ruff, which gives it its dressy style.

MATERIALS

- 1 spool of Madeira Sticku 30, in the following colours: green 1169, red 1038, blue 1024, beige 1084 and white 1071

- 1 x 4m (4⅓yd) packet of white gimp

- Mould, see page 153

- Reusable adhesive

- 3.25m (3½yd) of 0.37mm (0.014in) galvanized wire

- 1cm (⅜in) diameter wooden dowel

- Strong-impact adhesive

- Strong polyester thread

- 6mm knitting needle

- Hammer

- Standard equipment

Suspension cord: make a two-strand cord using two warps of 20 ends x 75cm (30in), in green and red, and one in blue and beige.

Mould: roll the mould with the white gimp – it will take just under 2m (2⅛yd).

Net: make a two-strand cord using two warps of 4 ends x 4m (4⅓yd) in red (see page 62 for method).

Skirt: make warps in each colour of 60 ends x 3.7m (4yd) over a 25cm (10in) board.

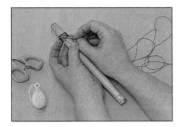

1 Start the net on the dowel, using the fine red cord. Make ten stitches round the dowel, and stitch five rows down (see page 62 for method).

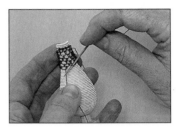

2 Transfer the net to the mould and continue stitching until you have covered the whole mould. Finish the net by looping through each stitch to make a drawstring and tighten.

3 Make the skirt very tightly. Twist the skirt wires, to prevent the ends coming loose, and glue them also. Attach the skirt and bind the waist a little.

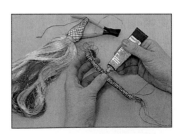

4 Make a ruff, using all the yarns together and 2m (2⅛yd) of wire, of 80 ends x 3m (3⅓yd) in all, on a 6mm knitting needle. You should have about 73 loops for the bottom ruff and 20 loops for the top ruff. Glue the spine of the ruffs and leave to dry.

5 Cut through the loops of both ruffs.

6 Attach the ruffs to the mould and stitch to secure.

7 Take the cord through the mould. To finish, make a tiny tuft in red yarn (see page 60). Open it out and hammer it flat, then trim. Glue in place, as shown.

Three-in-a-row Tassel

This delicate tassel is a beautiful decoration for a simply styled room, with off-white or lime-washed walls and natural fabric curtains. It is a brilliant and frivolous adaptation of tassel making techniques as the fringes round the shells are really cut ruffs. The rayon yarn and pearlescent paint set each other off perfectly. The shells must be all the same size, and need to fit together well as pairs. Once you have made this tassel, why not try attaching cut ruffs and skirts to larger conches or other round shells, to make a whole collection of imaginative seaside tassels?

MATERIALS

- 30g (1¼oz) of William Hall's 1200/2's rayon, in silver sand

- 3 pairs of shells

- White pearlescent acrylic paint

- 3m (3¼yd) of 0.37mm (0.014in) galvanized wire

- Strong clear glue

- Standard equipment

Suspension cord: make a two-strand cord using two warps of 10 ends x 80cm (32in) of silver-sand rayon. Knot or bind the ends to secure.

1 Apply a coat of pearlescent paint to the outside of all the shells.

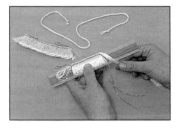

2 Make three warps of 30 ends x 1m (39in) for each shell. Using a 2.5cm (1in) board and 1m (39in) wire per ruff, make three ruffs.

3 Lay the shells out in matching pairs. Glue on the ruffs 5mm (¼in) inside one half of each shell. Leave to dry, then trim.

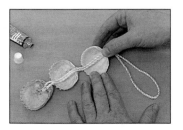

4 Knot the cord into a loop and glue it onto the shells, leaving a 1cm (½in) gap between each one.

5 Glue on the other halves of the shells. Place a book on top of the tassel until dry.

Jasmin Drops

This is a classic tassel for the most luxurious of drawing-rooms. It includes many of the techniques already covered in previous projects but these instructions concentrate on the bullion skirt, which is made of spun gimp and hung with drops made up of covered balls, gimp jasmins and flattened pompoms. Before you make the jasmin drops, cover the moulds and make the suspension cord in matching colours.

MATERIALS

- 1 cone of burgundy red gimp
- 1 spool of Madeira Tanne cotton 30, in green 575
- Moulds, see page 155
- Bobbin
- Masking tape
- 1.25m (1⅜yd) of 0.37mm (0.014in) galvanized wire
- Strong polyester thread
- 1.25mm (⅟₁₆in) diameter wooden dowel
- Strong-impact adhesive
- Hammer
- 30 x 1.25mm (⅟₁₆in) diameter wooden balls, with 3mm (⅛in) holes
- Button
- Standard equipment

Skirt: spin up the gimp outdoors, using a cuphook in a cordless electric drill. You will need 80m (87½yd) of gimp in all, so find a space long enough to spin four lengths x 20m (21¾yd). You will lose 12.5 per cent of the length in the spinning, ie 2.5m (2¾yd) of each length, and will end up with about 70m (76½yd) of spun gimp. Be careful not to let the tension slacken on the gimp as you spin. Wind the spun gimp carefully onto a bobbin or similar carrier, attaching the beginning to the bobbin with masking tape so that it cannot move. Knot the end of the first length onto the beginning of the second, and so on. Tape down the end of the last length so that the spin is not lost. Leave the spun gimp wound firmly on the bobbin until the next day before using it – the twist goes "dead" and it is easier to work.

1 Make the skirt on an 18cm (7¼in) board, winding the spun gimp very neatly and carefully at an angle.

2 Slide the bullions off the back of the board one by one, twisting them as you go, to make room at the front. Steam them over a boiling kettle to get the spin back in.

3 Thread the suspension cord wires through the covered moulds. Wind the skirt round the wires, and secure.

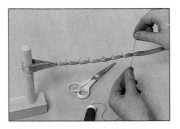

4 To make pompoms, wind 300 ends of the green cotton yarn round two posts, 75cm (30in) apart. Bind *very* tightly with polyester thread at 2.5cm (1in) intervals.

5 Cut between the bindings and open out the tufts. Hammer the pompoms firmly to flatten them. Trim.

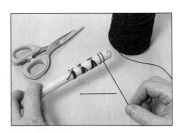

6 To make each jasmin, wind the gimp round the dowel five times, as shown. Stitch and knot polyester thread *tightly* around the five groups of gimps.

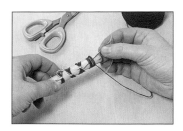

7 Cut the white threads and open out to make a four-leaf jasmin. Make five more jasmins the same way. Repeat three times.

8 Cover the balls with a warp of 20 ends x 10m (11yd), in green and red. String the balls and jasmins onto a fine two-strand cotton cord of 6 ends x 2.6m (2⅞yd) in green, with a knot at the bottom of each length of cord.

9 Arrange the balls and jasmins evenly round the skirt and stitch in. Thread a button onto the wires, glue the skirt into the tassel mould then twist up the wires with round-nosed pliers so that the skirt is secure.

Gold Silk Jasmin Tassel

*J*asmins were originally made by spinning silk yarn round a vellum strip, vellum being a strong but supple base that could easily be formed into these four-leaf shapes. This beautiful golden tassel uses gimp as a modern alternative. Make sure you bind the jasmins tightly so that they do not come loose. This is a delicate tassel and the jasmins may get squashed, so keep it in a special place.

MATERIALS

■ 1 spool of Madeira Decor, in gold 1525

■ Mould, see page 154

■ 5 x 4m (4¼yd) packets of pale gold gimp

■ 1cm (½in) diameter wooden dowel

■ Strong polyester thread

■ 5 beads

■ Clear glue

■ Standard equipment

Suspension cord: make a two-strand cord using one warp of 10 ends x 1.2m (1¼yd) of the Decor yarn. Twist up, loop around the warping post and onto the cabler and ply back. Knot the ends quickly.

Mould: cover the mould and beads using a warp of 10 ends x 1.2m (1¼yd) of the yarn.

Fine twine: make a two-strand cord using two warps of 2 ends x 2m (2¼yd), in the Decor yarn.

1 Knot the ends of the suspension cord, and thread it through the mould. To make the jasmins, wind the gimp round the dowel five times (see page 132).

2 Stitch through the gimp and bind very tightly. Continue until you finish the packet of gimp. Make five jasmins in the same way.

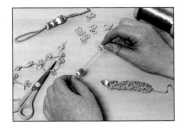

3 Snip the jasmins and flatten them out. String the jasmins onto the fine twine, and add a covered bead at the end of each string.

4 Bind the jasmins to the suspension cord very tightly. Glue the bindings.

5 Pull the whole lot up into the tassel mould.

Knotted Tie-back

Although this tassel tie-back looks very impressive, it is not difficult to make. The jute yarn is easy to use, looks crisp and neat, and sets off today's natural fabrics and interiors well. The embrace is long enough for quite a large, heavy curtain and you may need to shorten it a little. The size of the cord and the knot give the tie-back weight, and the total effect is very professional, giving your room a final handsome touch.

MATERIALS

- 400g (14oz) of fine jute (for one tie-back)
- Mould, see page 153
- 4m (4¼yd) of 0.37mm (0.014in) galvanized wire
- 5mm knitting needle
- Strong polyester thread
- 20cm (7¾in) of 1mm (0.04in) galvanized wire
- Button
- Standard equipment

Suspension cord: make a four-strand cabled cord using a large cuphook in a drill. Make eight warps, each 18 ends x 4m (4¼yd). Take the first pair and Z twist each strand only about half as tightly as for an ordinary cord, then S ply. Spin three more cords in the same way. Twist up each cord, continuing in the S direction. Z ply all four cords together, with a friend running knitting needles in front of the twist.

Mould: for each tassel, make two warps each of 3 ends x 3.5m (3¾yd).

Skirt: make a warp of 6 ends x 20m (21⅓yd), over an 18cm (7¼in) board.

Bottom ruff: make a warp of 18 ends x 2m (2¼yd), and make 80 loops on a 5mm knitting needle, using 1.8m (2yd) of 0.037mm (0.014in) galvanized wire.

Top ruff: make 15 loops on a 5mm knitting needle from the end of the warp, using 1m (39in) of wire.

Over-bullions: make six small warps of 60cm (24in) each. S twist each warp, fold and Z ply. Bind the cut ends.

1 For the tufts, wind the jute round your fingers 36 times. Thread the bundle through the loop at the end of the over-bullion. Fold it over and bind.

2 Attach the skirt to the mould then place the first over-bullion onto the tassel and bind in. Continue to place and bind all six over-bullions.

3 For the embrace knot, make an "M" shape with the suspension cord over the warping post.

4 Take the left-hand end of the cord over the centre and round.

5 This will make a loop. Twist the loop.

6 Take the end through the loop as shown.

Continued overleaf

7 Take the right-hand cord over the centre and round.

8 This will make another loop. Twist the loop.

9 Pull the cord through in the same way as for the first loop.

10 Place a loop of 1mm (0.04in) wire through the cord and bind tightly.

11 Attach the bottom ruff to the tassel, then take the wires through the tassel. Next thread the button onto the wires. Twist up the wires tightly through the button, using round-nosed pliers. Attach the top ruff.

Left: Here a bullion skirt is combined with a flat mould. Flat moulds, first used as ceremonial regalia, are now fashionable for tie-backs.

Turk's Head Knot

*A*nd now for a Turk's head knot! This tassel is made from crewel embroidery wool so the knot is nice and chunky. The cord is "double-spun and plain" ie there are two cabled (or double-spun) strands in red/yellow and beige/yellow, and two plain strands, blue and olive-green. Make the double-spun strands first, then spin them up together with the plain strands. Make the Turk's head knot larger than the cord it is to go on as the spaces will be eaten up as you form the knot – by the time you have finished threading the cord, the knot will be quite large.

MATERIALS

- 1 x 25g (1oz) hank of Appleton's crewel embroidery wool, in the following colours: madder red 866, yellow 474, beige 692, olive green 314 and indigo blue 324

- Mould, see page 155

- Reusable adhesive

- 1.2m (1¼yd) of 0.37mm (0.014in) galvanized wire

- Strong polyester thread

- Tapestry needle

- Button

- Standard equipment

Suspension cord: make a double-spun and plain cord using six warps, one each of 15 ends x 1.2m (1¼yd) in red and yellow and beige and yellow, then one each of 30 ends x 1m (39in) in olive green and blue. S spin softly and then Z ply together the red and yellow, then do the same with the beige and yellow. Z spin together with the olive green and blue. S ply the whole lot together using knitting needles (see step 1).

Twine: make a two-strand cord using two warps of 8 ends x 4.25m (4½yd) in red.

Mould: make a two-strand cord of 8 ends x 4m (4¼yd) in yellow. Roll the mould.

Skirt: using olive green, make 20 ends x 40 tags on a 26cm (10½in) skirt board.

1 Use needles to keep the colour sequence when S plying all the cords together.

2 Bind the cord into a loop, leaving 25cm (10in) at one end.

3 Cut off that length of cord, fold it over the loop and bind quickly.

4 Bind the join with red wool until it forms a spherical base for the Turk's head knot. Form a loop in the middle of the twine.

5 Make a second loop, holding the two loops between your thumb and first finger.

6 Then take the end of the twine and thread it through the loops.

7 Weave it *over, under, over, under* the two loops until it looks like this.

Continued overleaf

8 The twine should now look like this.

9 Thread a tapestry needle with one end of the twine and follow through the knot in the same sequence as in step 7.

10 The twine should look like this now.

11 Slip the knot carefully over the cord and form it over the bound knob.

12 Carefully stitch through the knot, again following the same sequence and keeping the same tension. Make about three complete revolutions.

13 Thread the other end of the twine, and take it again through the sequence until it has completely closed all the space left at the beginning. Stitch the ends of the twines into the ball of the knot. Make a hairpin of wire, thread it through the cord end, and take it through the mould. Wrap the skirt round the cord and thread the wires through a button. Twist up the wires to secure the skirt and mould.

Ecru Silk Tassel Tie-back

This is another way of making a tie-back, this time using a covered mould to hold the embrace together instead of a knot. The skirt tags are hung alternately with pompoms and corded tufts, and the mould is rolled with a twine alongside a gimp. The effect is a rich combination of textures, accentuated by the lustre in the silk. The silk comes in 250g (8oz) cones, and one will be enough for the tassel, even though a lot of yarn is used for the cord.

MATERIALS

- 1 cone Texere undyed silk 2/27's SS30 per tie-back

- 1 x 4m (4¼yd) packet of ecru gimp per tie-back

- 1.2m (1¼yd) 0.37mm (0.014in) galvanized wire

- Moulds, see page 152

- Strong-impact adhesive

- Strong polyester thread

- 20cm (7⅞in) of 1mm (0.04in) galvanized wire

- Button

- Standard equipment

Suspension cord: make a three-strand cabled cord using three warps of 50 ends x 4m (4¼yd) of silk. Cable the strands Z, then ply the whole lot together S. (This will give you enough cord so that you can cut off the end nearest the cordspinner, which sometimes does not spin up quite as tightly as the far end.)

Moulds: make a fine two-strand cord using two warps of 4.2m (4½yd) x 12 ends.

Skirt: use 30 ends x 17.5m (19yd) of silk on a 12cm (4¾in) skirt board.

Cord tassels: make a two-strand cord of 6 ends of silk wound four times round a 7mm (⅜in) skirt board.

Pompoms: use 100 ends of silk, bound at 2cm (¾in) intervals. Leave enough of the binding thread to tie the pompoms onto the skirt tags.

1 Cover the embrace mould with 30 ends x 1.3m (1⅓yd) and bind with fine silk twine. Thread the suspension cord through the covered mould as shown.

2 Roll the tassel mould with 2m (2¼yd) of ecru gimp and the fine silk cord.

3 Tie a pompom, alternating with a tassel, onto each pair of tags on the skirt.

4 Bind a loop of 1mm (0.04in) galvanized wire to the suspension cord endings.

5 Thread these wires through the tassel mould, then wind the skirt round.

6 Twist up the skirt wires to tighten them.

7 Thread a button onto the thick cord wires and twist them up with pliers.

Scarf with Bead Tassel Ends

The tassels made for this scarf are similar in construction to the Bead Skirt Tassel on page 122. The grey and black cotton yarns are ordinary 50s sewing threads, slightly finer than the 30s yarns used for the other projects. They look very smart with the steely blue-grey fabric. Look for beads with large holes as smaller holes fill up with the yarn covering. See page 149 for instructions on how to attach the rosette and tassel to the scarf.

MATERIALS

- 1 x 500m (547yd) spool of Sylko 50, in grey and black
- Mould, see page 152
- Hammer
- Strong polyester thread
- 24 beads
- 2m (2¼yd) of 0.37mm (0.014in) galvanized wire
- Buckram and pencil
- Strong-impact adhesive
- 2mm knitting needle
- Standard equipment

Suspension cord: make a two-strand cord using one warp of 20 ends x 2m (2¼yd) in black. Loop the warp over the post and onto the cabler and spin up.

Fine cord: make a two-strand cord using two warps of 6 ends x 1m (39in) in black. Cut in half and bind the ends.

Mould: make a warp of 20 ends x 1m (39in) in mixed grey and black yarn.

Beads: make a warp of 20 ends x 4m (4¼yd) x 20 ends in grey yarn.

Tufts: to make 16 tufts, place the posts 30cm (12in) apart. Wind black yarn on the posts to give 200 ends. Bind at 1cm (½in) intervals. Cut in between each binding. Press the tufts open and hammer.

Ruffs: use 20 ends x 20cm (7¾in) of black yarn and 1m (39in) of wire.

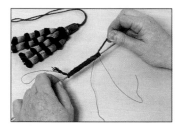

1 Cover the mould and the beads. Thread eight beads and eight tufts onto each fine cord. Thread the suspension cord through the mould and catch the two fine cords. Pull them up into the mould.

2 For the rosette, make a ruff of 42 loops x 40 ends of black yarn on a 2mm knitting needle and using 1m (39in) of wire.

3 Draw a circle on a piece of buckram. Cut through the rosette ruff.

4 Spiral the ruff into a circle to make the rosette. Twist the beginning and end wires together.

5 Apply glue to the circle of buckram.

6 Stick the buckram onto the back of the rosette.

7 Make a hole in the rosette with fine-pointed scissors. Thread the tassel cord through, and knot the end.

Rosette

These French tassels are pretty and feminine. They are mainly found in 18th-century interiors, and if you study them you can see the natural dyes that were used – pale madder pinks, indigo blues and greens made from natural yellows on top of indigo. This rosette is made of pale pink, ivory and sage green gimp, and an indigo blue ruff. The technique used here is simply a crochet chain – the idea is to chain the gimps without crossing them over each other, and then to make an invisible join. Place the rosette on a tassel in matching colours.

MATERIALS

- 2 x 4m (4¼yd) packets of gimp, in pink, ivory and green

- 1 spool of Madeira Sticku, in blue 1028 and pink 1317

- Strong polyester thread

- Strong-impact adhesive glue

- 1.1m (42in) of 0.37mm (0.014in) galvanized wire

- Button

- Circle of buckram

- Standard equipment

1 To make the rosette, bind the three gimps together and make a loop.

2 Keep turning the gimps in a circle, then pull this second loop through the first.

3 Tighten up by pulling the inside, middle and then the outside gimp.

4 The first two loops create a shape like this. Start on the third loop.

5 On the eleventh loop, pull the ends of the gimps through.

6 Bind the ends, and push them through the first loop to form a circle.

7 Tie the ends together. Cover the rosette button using 20 ends x 1m (39in) of pink 1317. Make a ruff of 60 ends of blue, and form into a circle to enclose the button.

8 Glue the ruff and button onto the rosette. Glue the buckram circle to the back of the rosette, pierce it with scissors and pull the cord of your chosen tassel through.

Applications of Cords and Tassels

Now that tassels and trimmings have again become fashionable, people decorating their own homes and interior decorators are starting to commission new work from trimmings workshops, or to buy the exciting ranges now *available from the better department stores and interior decoration shops. Here are instructions for how to apply the tassels and trimmings in the projects to cushions, bolsters and scarves.*

ATTACHING A CORD TO A CUSHION COVER

1 Bind the cord at the end and also about 7cm (2¾in) in. Carefully untwist the cord between the bindings and stitch to the wrong side of the cushion cover at an angle of 45°.

2 Measure the exact amount of cord needed to go round the cushion cover, and add 7cm (2¾in) extra. Bind the end, then bind again 7cm (2¾in) in. Now untwist, and stitch at an 180° angle to the beginning of the cord. Make sure that the colour sequence runs in order.

3 Unravel the ends of the cord. Stitch the back and front of the cushion cover together with a seam allowance 3mm (⅛in) or so inside that first stitching. Trim the cord ends.

4 Turn to the right side of the cushion and snip off the bindings.

5 You now have an invisible join. Stitch the cord onto the outside of the cushion.

Left: A cushion cover knitted in basketweave stitch with tassels to match

ATTACHING A TASSEL TO A SCARF

1 Fold a length of silk 1.5m x 50cm (1¾yd x 20in) to make a self-backed scarf 1.5m x 25cm (1¾yd x 10in). Stitch the outside seams on the wrong side, then turn the tube to the right side and press. Pleat the end of the scarf.

2 Holding the end of the pleat together with a clothes peg, stitch through to secure.

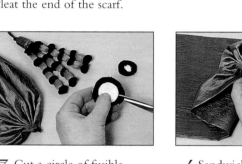

3 Cut a circle of fusible buckrum, 3cm (1⅛in) diameter, and cover with a 5cm (2in) circle of black velvet. Iron together. You will need two velvet discs, one for each end of the scarf.

4 Sandwich the scarf end between the rosette and the velvet disc, and stitch together securely round the edge. Stab stitch through the middle.

Above: Specially designed to co-ordinate with the design of the print, these tassels add a classical-cum-oriental touch, and give weight to the scarf.

ATTACHING A ROSETTE AND TASSEL TO A BOLSTER

1 Stab a hole through the button of the bolster with a pair of scissors.

2 Thread the tassel cord through a covered disc of buckrum and then through the bolster button.

3 Pull the cord inside the bolster cover and secure with a knot inside the bolster. Stitch the disc onto the button.

4 Glue the rosette onto the disc, using strong-impact adhesive.

Glossary

Bullion *As in bullion or skirt fringe. The technique of twisting up yarn so tightly that it spins back on itself forming a loop with an uncut edge.*

Cabling *Strands that have already been spun and plied before being made up into a multi-strand cord.*

Cord *A set of yarns that are spun together to form a thicker length. Cords are used to suspend the tassel, or as decoration on the mould or skirt (see also Basic Techniques).*

Covering *A technique for decorating the mould in which the mould is covered vertically with a warp (see also Basic Techniques).*

Crewel embroidery *Decorative stitching using fine worsted thread.*

Découpage *A decorative technique in which ornamental motifs are cut out of printed paper and are stuck onto a surface.*

Double-spun *See Cabling above.*

Drops *Beads, jasmins and/or tufts strung together and suspended from a mould over the tassel skirt.*

Embrace *The cord that surrounds the curtain in a tie-back, from which tassels are suspended.*

Ends *Each warp is made up of a certain number of threads, and each thread is an end.*

Gimp *Silk, wool or cotton yarn that is wound round a core of cheaper threads or wire.*

Jasmin *Four-leaf floret formed out of gimp, or vellum, usually strung together to form a drop.*

Mould *Wooden form used as the basis of the construction of a tassel.*

Netting *Detached buttonhole stitching used to decorate a tassel mould.*

Niddy-noddy *A tool used by spinners to wind handspun yarn off the bobbin of the spinning wheel into a skein.*

Over-bullion *Thicker cords positioned over a tassel skirt, often carrying a tuft.*

Parandah *A brightly coloured set of cords, or yarns, plaited into the hair. Used by women in India as a plait extension.*

Plying *This is when two or more strands are twisted together to form one cord.*

Rolling *A technique for decorating a tassel mould. The mould is first covered in glue and then wound in a spiral with a gimp or fine cord (see also Basic Techniques).*

Ruff *Ruffs are wound around a tassel to hide the joins between a suspension cord and mould, and a mould and skirt. They also provide a focal point.*

Skirt *The fringing that forms the bottom of the tassel.*

Snailing *A technique for embellishing the mould. Gimps, vellums or cords are crossed around the tassel mould, going over and under each other.*

Squab *A squab tassel is pulled up to create a squashed effect.*

Striping *A decorative technique using cords laid vertically on a tassel mould.*

Tag *The loops of yarn or bullion that form the skirt; one loop is one tag.*

Trellising *A decorative technique on the tassel skirt, whereby yarns are criss-crossed and bound.*

Tufts *A small tassel used to decorate the skirt of a larger tassel.*

Vellum *A flat strip covered with good-quality yarn, used for decorating tassels. Vellum was originally made from calf's skin which is very strong but pliable.*

Warp *A group of threads prepared in a given length which are used for the cord, skirt, ruffs or for covering the mould.*

Whipping *A cordspinning technique in which strands are spiralled with gimp before being spun into a cord*

Opposite: These innovative tassels show some of the interesting materials that can be used when designing and making skirts.

Templates

Most of the tassels made in this book use moulds. Some of the moulds are made out of paper or adapted from other items such as curtain finials or large beads. For others they are specially-made tassel moulds. These can either be bought by mail-order from Anna Crutchley or you can ask a wood turner to make them for you. Your local hardware store should be able to put you in touch with a wood turner. These are the templates for the moulds and they are reproduced at their actual size. The dotted lines indicate the area to be carved out.

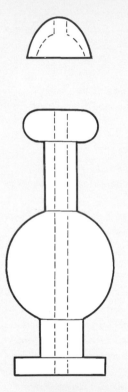

Trellised tassel, page116

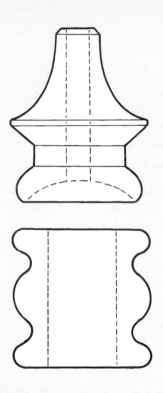

Ecru silk tassel tie-back, page 142

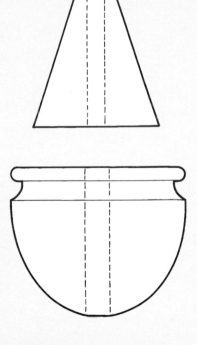

Indigo drop tassel, page 80

Tiny pompom tassel, page 84 and scarf with bead tassel ends, page 144

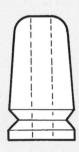

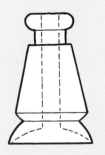

Tartan drawstring bag, page 108

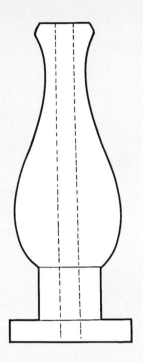

Green jute tassel, page 58

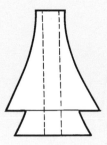

Two-level bullion
tassel, page 110

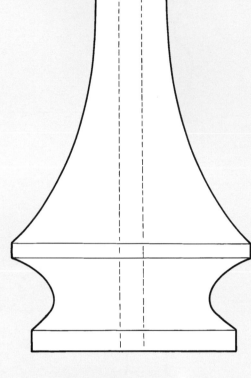

Knotted tie-back, page 137

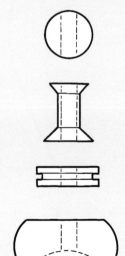

Gold silk jasmin tassel, page 134

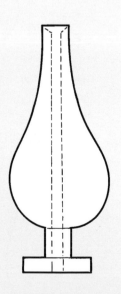

Tassel with cut ruff, page 128

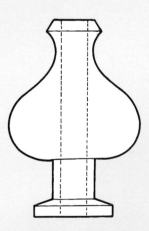

Snailed tassel, page 87

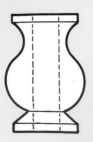

Panelled skirt tassel,
page 96

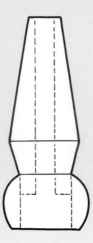

Loop skirt tassel, page 74
and tufted tassel, page 114

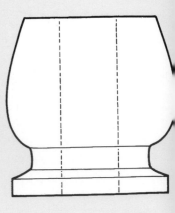

Linen tassel, page 112

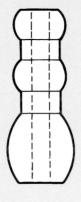

Gold silk jasmin tassel,
page 134

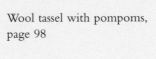

Wool tassel with pompoms,
page 98

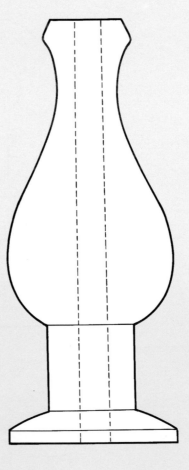

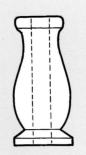

Dip-dyed silk tassel,
page 100

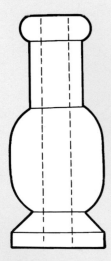

Jute tassel, page 60

Bead skirt tassel,
page 122

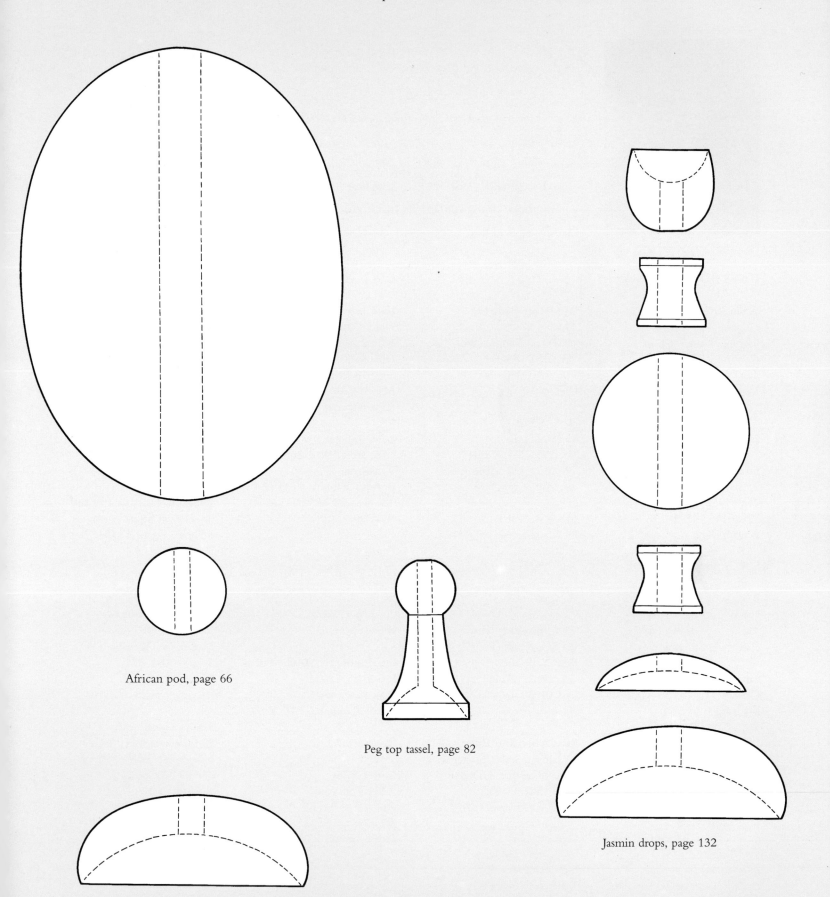

African pod, page 66

Peg top tassel, page 82

Jasmin drops, page 132

Turk's head knot, page 139

Stockists

The yarns that are to be used for each tassel are listed by each project. The Sylko sewing thread, strong polyester thread and crotchet cottons can be bought in any good department store. For most of the other materials you will need to contact the specialist supplier. Listed below are main suppliers in each country. If, however, you would like further information, please contact the head offices or main supplier of each brand. These addresses also listed below.

UNITED KINGDOM

William Hall & Co
177 Stanley Road
Cheadle Hume, Cheadle
Cheshire SK8 6RF
Tel/Fax: 0161 437 3295
Bocken's linens and
William Hall yarns

Fibrecrafts
Style Cottage
Lower Eashing, Godalming
Surrey GU7 2QD
Tel: 01483 421853
Fax: 01483 419960
Borg's linens

Silken Strands
20 Y Rhos
Bangor LL57 2LT
Tel/Fax: 01248 362361
Madeira threads and Bourdon cords and gimp yarns

Texere Yarns
College Mill, Barkerend Road
Bradford BD3 9AQ
Tel: 01274 722191
Fax: 01274 393500
Texere yarns

Anna Crutchley
The Frater Studio
6B Priory Road
Cambridge CB5 8HT
Tel: 01223 327685
Jute and wooden moulds, special orders of cotton gimp and cordspinners

Appleton Bros Ltd
Thames Works, Church Street
Chiswick, London W4 2PE
Tel: 0181 994 0711
Fax: 0181 995 6609
Appleton's wools

W H I Ltd
85 Pimlico Road
London SW1 W8PH
Tel: 0171 730 5366
Appleton's wools

Mace & Nairn
89 Crane Street, Salisbury
Wiltshire SP1 2PY
Tel: 01722 336903
Fax: 01722 416397
Appleton's wools

The Spinning Jenny
Bradley, Keighley
West Yorkshire BD20 9DD
Tel: 01535 632469
Fax: 01535 636431
Appleton's wools

Miss Christine Riley
53 Barclay Street, Stonehaven
Kincardineshire AB3 2AR
Tel: 01569 763238
Appleton's wools

Leanda
39 Borrowdale Drive
Norwich NR1 4LY
Tel/Fax: 01603 434707
Warping posts, frames and boards

CANADA

June Hanson
Nordic Studio
R R 2 Lunenburg
Ontario KOC 1RO
Tel: 613 346 2373
Fax: 613 346 0103
Bocken's linens

Dick and Jane
2352 West 41st Avenue
Vancouver
British Columbia V6M 2A4
Tel: 604 738 3574
Appleton's wools

Fancyworks
104-3960 Quera Street
Victoria
British Columbia V8X 4A3
Tel: 604 727 2765
Appleton's wools

Jet Handcraft Studio Ltd
P O Box 91103
West Vancouver
British Columbia V7V 3N3
Tel: 604 922 8820
Appleton's wools

Louet Sales
RR – 4 Prescott
Ontario KOE ITP
Tel: 613 925 4502
Warping frames

AUSTRALIA

Glenora Crafts
Sth Avondale Road
2530 Dapto
Tel: 042 61 5099
Bocken's linens

Petlin Industries
P S Box 76, North Richmond
New South Wales 2754
Tel: 02 8051676
Borgs's linens

Penguin Threads Pty Ltd
25-27 Izett Street
Prahran, Victoria 3181
Tel: 0395 294400
Madeira threads and yarns

**Clifton H Joseph & Son
(Australia) Pty Ltd**
391-393 Little Lonsdale Street
Melbourne, Victoria 3000
Tel: 03 96021222
Fax: 03 96000929
Appleton's wools

Stadia Handicrafts
85 Elizabeth Street, Paddington
New South Wales 2021
Tel: 02 328 7973
Appleton's wools

P L Stonewall & Co Pty Ltd
52 Erskine Street
Sydney, NSW
Tel: 02 2994271
Appleton's wools

NEW ZEALAND

Glenora Craft
P O Box 313
Picton
Tel: 03 5736966
Bocken's linens

Nancy's Embroidery Ltd
326 Tinakori Road
P O Box 245
Thorndon, Wellington
Tel: 04 473 4047
Appleton's wools

FURTHER INFORMATION

For further information or addresses about a specific material, contact the head office of the company concerned.

BOCKEN'S LINENS
Holma–Helsinglands AB
Box 1, S–820 65 Forsa
Sweden
Tel: 650 231 01
Fax: 650 236 09

BORG'S LINEN
Borgs Vavgarner AB
Box 14, Vittsjo, Sweden
Tel: 451 22900
Fax: 451 23375

WILLIAM HALL YARNS
William Hall & Co
177 Stanley Road
Cheadle Hume, Cheshire
SK8 6 RF England
Tel/Fax: 0161 437 3295

APPLETON YARNS
Appleton Bros Ltd
Thames Works
Church Street, Chiswick
London W4 2PE England
Tel: 0181 994 0711
Fax: 0181 995 6609

MADEIRA THREADS
Barnyarns Ltd
PO Box 28
Thirsk, North Yorkshire
YO7 3YN England
Tel: 01845 524344
World-wide mail order

GIMPS
Silken Strands
20 Y Rhos
Bangor
LL57 2LT England
Tel/Fax: 01248 362361

GENERAL EQUIPMENT
Leanda
39 Borrowdale Drive
Norwich NR1 4LY
Tel/Fax: 01603 434707

Below: Lakai bag.

ndex

numbers in italic refer to illustrations

$\mathcal{A}$ c k n o w l e d g e m e n t s

The art of passementerie takes many years to master; I would not have had the chance to start learning this fascinating craft without the first commissions from Joy King and Mary Wondrausch, the goodwill of Brian Turner and the weavers and tassel makers at Turners Trimmings Ltd, and Stan Leaning's generosity in teaching me to spin cord.

For the book I would like to thank the students on the B.A. Honours course in Floor Covering and Interior Textiles at Kidderminster College, their tutors, and in particular, Janet Oliver. Their projects in the book are inventive and refreshing, and add scope to contemporary tassel design. I would also like to thank Lucy Tizard for the step photography, and Anna Tait and Tim Imrie for their exceptional photography; Clare Nicholson at Anness Publishing for her scrupulous organisation; Judy Walker and Alison Hennegan who helped with the text; Heidi Lichterman and Gillian Wightman for helping make the tassels, and for their positive criticism; Kate Hallam who skilfully stitched the fabrics into bags and cushions; Michael Leslie for keeping my life in order and John Leigh for always being at the end of the line to help with computer queries, even when he was in America.

PICTURE CREDITS

The publishers and author would like to thank the following people for the work in contributing projects for the book: Lynn Knowles, page 64; Lyn Shimwell, pages 76 and 92; Juliet Harris, page 78; Georgina Downward, pages 94 and 102; Kim Cockett, page 89; Zoe Barlow, page 118; Vikki Atkins, pages 120 and 130. They would also like to thank the following people for their generosity in loaning tassels for photography:

Guy Evans, 96 Great Titchfield Street, London W1P 7AG (tel: 0171 436 7914/5), for the tassels on pages 9, 14r, 15 (2nd left) and 51.

Wendy Cushing Trimmings, Unit M7 Chelsea Garden Market, Chelsea Harbour, London SW10 OXE (tel: 0171 351 5776), for the tassels on pages 16, 23t, 32 and 68.

Wemyss Houles, 40 Newman Street, London W1P 3PA (tel: 0171 255 3305), for the tassels on pages 19, 24, 28, 70tl, 71 and 138.

Frances Souberyan, 12 Atlas Mews, Ramsgate Street, London E8 2NE (tel: 0171 241 1064), for the tassels on pages 15 (right and far right), 22, 23bl, 70tr, 107 and 113.

Percheron, 97-99 Cleveland Street, London W1P 5PN (tel: 0171 580 1192), for the tassels on the front and back cover.

Anna Crutchley, The Frater Studio, 6B Priory Road, Cambridge, CB5 8HT (tel: 01223 327685), for pages 8b, 15 (l and c), 18, 26, 25, 51tr, 51b, 104, 106b, 106t, 124, 126t, 126bl, 126br and 127.

Alistair Hull, 18A High Street, Haddenham, Ely, Cambridgeshire CB6 3TA for the tassels on pages 8t, 10, 11 and 70b.

Stan Leaning for the cords on pages 48 and 50.

Lynn Knowles, Passementerie Designer, 15 Cumberland Close, Kingswinford, DY6 8JE, for the tassels on page 17.

The students of Kidderminster College, for the tassels on page 150.

Crispian Steele Perkins, for the trumpets on page 25.

The tassel on page 12 was photographed by gracious permission of Her Majesty The Queen. The pictures on pages 13 and 141 were reproduced by kind permission of E.T. Archive, and the picture on page 27t was reproduced by kind permission of The Fan Museum, Greenwich. The photograph on page 20 is by Graham Rae and the photograph on page 23r is by Debbie Patterson.